Other Books You May Enjoy

Anne Frank and the Children of the Holocaust	*Carol Ann Lee*
The Boys in the Boat (Adapted for Young Readers)	*Daniel James Brown*
Brown Girl Dreaming	*Jacqueline Woodson*
Code Talker	*Joseph Bruchac*
How I Discovered Poetry	*Marilyn Nelson*
Jack: The Early Years of John F. Kennedy	*Ilene Cooper*
Margaret Mead: The World Was Her Family (Women of Our Time)	*Susan Saunders*
Rachel Carson: Pioneer of Ecology (Women of Our Time)	*Kathleen V. Kudlinski*
They Did What? 50 Impressive Kids and Their Amazing (and True!) Stories	*Saundra Mitchell*
They Did What? 50 Incredible Women and Their Fascinating (and True!) Stories	*Saundra Mitchell*

TEN DAYS
a MADWOMAN

TEN DAYS
a MADWOMAN

The Daring Life and Turbulent Times of the
Original "Girl" Reporter, **Nellie Bly**

DEBORAH NOYES

PUFFIN BOOKS

PUFFIN BOOKS
An imprint of Penguin Random House LLC
375 Hudson Street
New York, New York 10014

First published in the United States of America by Viking, an imprint of Penguin Random House LLC, 2016
Published by Puffin Books, an imprint of Penguin Random House LLC, 2017

THE LIBRARY OF CONGRESS HAS CATALOGED THE VIKING EDITION AS FOLLOWS:
Noyes, Deborah.
Ten days a madwoman : the daring life and turbulent times of the
original "girl" reporter Nellie Bly / Deborah Noyes.
pages cm
ISBN: 978-0-8037-4017-4 (hardback)
1. Bly, Nellie, 1864 – 1922—Juvenile literature.
2. Journalists—United States—Biography—Juvenile literature.
3. Women journalists—United States—Biography—Juvenile Literature.
I. Title.
PN4874.C59N65 2016
070.92—dc23
[B]
2015028368

Puffin Books ISBN 9780147508744

Printed in the United States of America

Designed by Kate Renner

3 5 7 9 10 8 6 4 2

CONTENTS

—✳—

MORNING PAPERS.

1: the GODS of GOTHAM

Dear Q.O.,

I am off for New York. Look out for me.

Bly

When the ambitious young reporter Elizabeth Jane "Pink" Cochran—known to her readers as Nellie Bly—left her life and family behind in Pittsburgh, Pennsylvania, she was confident one of New York City's major daily newspapers would hire her at once. She had spunk. She had experience. She was fearless and eager to learn.

And she was wrong.

Nellie left her mother, Mary Jane, behind in Pittsburgh on a May day in 1887, promising to send for her when she found steady work. She stepped up onto a train and later stepped down into the most populous city in the nation wearing a flowered hat she had bought while reporting in Mexico. Like thousands of other young hopefuls, twenty-three-year-old Nellie Bly was on her own for the first time in her life.

She rented a tiny furnished room overlooking an alley on West Ninety-Sixth Street. Her lodgings were in the northernmost part of settled Manhattan, where Broadway became Western Boulevard, and the "boulevard" wasn't paved yet. Goats wandered through, nibbling weeds in vacant lots between squat houses. It was about as far from where Nellie needed to be every day as it could get.

Left: An 1882 caricature of New York City's major morning newspaper publishers.

Her destination was Park Row, also known as Newspaper Row, a street slanting northeast from lower Broadway where newspaper offices hunkered along one side near City Hall. The trek downtown each day was epic. Nellie rode a steam locomotive a half hour south on the Ninth Avenue Elevated Railway. Then she walked east on streets where people lived grimly packed together in tenements (and were often "roasted," as newspaper reports of the day liked to put it, in devastating blazes). Typhus, cholera, and influenza swept through the area at regular intervals. Gambling dens and bordellos thrived while the police looked the other way. Robbery and murder were commonplace, keeping city reporters on their toes. The streets were a hazard in their own right. One of thousands of horses hauling the city's carts, carriages, hansom cabs, omnibuses, and streetcars might bolt at any moment, their transports careening into bystanders.

Nellie pounded the Park Row pavement in vain. The gatekeepers at the *Tribune*, the *Times*, the *Sun*, the *World*, the *Herald*, and the *Mail and Express*, who turned away aspiring reporters every day, were unimpressed by her Pittsburgh portfolio.

To scrape by that first summer in New York, Nellie wrote freelance articles for her old newspaper, the *Pittsburgh Dispatch*, where she had made her start and a (literal) name for herself. They were the sort of Sunday style stories she hated, about the rage for puffed sleeves among fashionable New York women, for example.

Around the time that her money and patience were beginning to run out, the *Dispatch* forwarded a letter from a young Pittsburgh woman. An aspiring journalist wanted Nellie's advice: Was New York the place to get a start? Could a woman writer make her mark there?

Nellie must have wanted to laugh out loud at the irony. But then an idea struck. What if she called on the editors of New York's six most influential newspapers, on behalf of the *Dispatch*, to harvest their thoughts on this very subject? She would "obtain the opinion of the newspaper gods of Gotham" and, at the same time, gain audience with the men who held her future in their ink-stained hands.

The first paper she visited was the *Sun*. As she climbed the dim spiral staircase to the third-floor newsroom with its haze of cigar smoke and raucous conversation, anxious office boys darted here and there on errands. In the summer heat, men would have removed their suit coats and vests, working in sweat-stained white shirts with high celluloid collars and rolled sleeves.

Her entrance must have caused a stir. Female reporters were still comparatively rare, even in big cities like New York and Pittsburgh—Nellie proved the exception to this and other rules—and there were likely no other women in the newsroom that day when she was escorted into the office of the paper's formidable editor and publisher, Charles A. Dana.

Between his reputation for hiring college men and his flowing Father Time beard—backed by a stuffed owl looking down from a shelf of reference books—Dana must have cut an imposing figure to a hungry "girl reporter." But after flushing out his stance on the topic with a few questions, Nellie asked, boldly, "Are you opposed to women as journalists, Mr. Dana?"

Top: Charles A. Dana around 1890. Bottom: City room of the New York World *around 1900.*

Certainly not, he objected. But "while a woman might be ever so clever in obtaining news and putting it into words," he said, "we would not feel at liberty to call her out at one o'clock in the morning to report at a fire or a crime. . . . [w]e never hesitate with a man."

Women also, he maintained, "find it impossible not to exaggerate."

Nellie soldiered on: "How do women secure positions in New York?"

She thought she saw a twinkle in his eye as he replied, "I really cannot say."

Nellie continued along Park Row with her questions. The editor of the *Herald* informed Nellie that for better or worse the public wanted scandal and sensation, "and a gentleman could not in delicacy ask a woman to have anything to do with that class of news."

The *Times* editor had never felt compelled to take up the topic with his colleagues.

Mr. Coates of the *Mail and Express* called women "invaluable." The way they dressed and their "constitution" ruled out hard reporting, but they were ideally equipped to cover stories on society, fashion, and gossip.

Women were "more ambitious than men," the editor at the *Telegram* echoed, "and had more energy," but he "couldn't very well send a woman out on a story where she might have to slide down a banister. . . . That's where a man gets the best of her."

BECOMING NELLIE BLY

Women journalists didn't publish under their real names in the late 1800s, when young Elizabeth Jane "Pink" Cochran started out at a salary of five dollars a week. To do so was unladylike. So when she joined the staff of the *Pittsburgh Dispatch*, her first editor, George Madden, called for a made-up "pen name." Other notable female reporters of the day went by the likes of "Bessie Bramble," "Fanny Fern," and "Penelope Penfeather," and Madden wanted something equally "neat

At the *New York World*, Colonel John Cockerill complained that women didn't want to write the fashion and society stories they were best fit for. "A man is of far greater service," he said in his forthright way, though he also claimed to have a couple of women on staff. "So you see, we do not object personally."

After weighing the words of these six powerful men, Nellie summed up their views: "We have more women now than we want. . . . Women are no good, anyway." Her article, "Women Journalists," traveled out from Pittsburgh to New York and Boston and received notice in *The Journalist*, a national trade magazine. Her choice of subject matter was a brilliant

strategy: it put Nellie Bly in the right place at almost the right time. Her moment was coming. But she had to hit rock bottom first.

Title page of Stephen Foster's musical score for "Nelly Bly."

and catchy" for his new hire. He set the newsroom pondering and, as legend has it, an office boy strolled past during the debate whistling a popular tune by Pittsburgh composer Stephen Foster about an African American servant named Nelly Bly. With an editor upstairs hollering for copy, Madden made his choice.

He spelled it wrong for the typesetter—"Nellie" instead of "Nelly"—but the name took, and it suited: Nellie Bly the reporter would go on to write about underprivileged women like her namesake throughout her long career.

PINK

MAY 5, 1864

In the dense thickets of Virginia known as the Wilderness of Spotsylvania, armies clashed in a bloody battle of the American Civil War. But three hundred miles to the north in rural Cochran's Mills, Pennsylvania, birthplace of the infant Elizabeth Jane Cochran—who grew up to circle the globe and report on the first global war—life was uneventful. It was a mild spring day. The woods blazed with violets. Wild turkey bobbed in greening fields where farmers raised corn, oats, and buckwheat. Miners coaxed slate, limestone, and coal from the ground.

Ordinary though her daughter's birthplace and circumstances were, Mary Jane Cochran soon decided—or observed—that this child, her third and her husband's thirteenth, would not be ordinary. While other little girls wore drab gray calico and basic brown, Mary Jane dressed hers in showy, starched pink with frills and white stockings. People took to calling the child Pink.

How did Pink, who liked chewing gum and horses, spend her early years in rural western Pennsylvania?

There were chores, of course, and, once her loving and affluent father moved the family to nearby Apollo, school. The town's lone schoolhouse, a two-story white-frame building boasting two teachers, one for primary and another for high school, was a short walk from home. Mr. Davis, who taught the older students upstairs, directed naughty boys—the sort who carved up the school's white-pine desks with broken pen points—down to the ravine in Owens' Woods to cut willow switches for their own punishment.

Pink distinguished herself as a scholar by smuggling friends into her father's library, where she hefted a big medical reference book from the shelf and astounded them with its racy contents.

In winter, there was sledding and skating. In summer, kids rolled barrel hoops down the hill to the canal bridge. They stood in line for penny candy at the general store and fished for carp in the Kiskiminetas River.

Pink may have run hollering through the rickety covered wooden bridge to hear the echo of her own voice, or dodged sheep and cattle driven through town toward the East Liberty Stockyards. She may have jumped rope, rocked a rag doll to sleep, or played mumblety-peg, paddleball, and marbles.

She probably looked on, wide-eyed, with other furtive young witnesses while storekeeper John Bar bought up the frogs the older boys caught on order, stunned his slippery victims with a blow to the head in the back alley, and lopped off their hind legs for shipment to Pittsburgh restaurants.

Frogs notwithstanding, it seems an almost idyllic small-town American childhood, though it would end too soon.

2: **MORE** than anyone would **BELIEVE**

> Write up things as you find them, good or bad; give praise or blame as you think best, and the truth all the time.

One fateful day in September, about four months into her New York adventure, Nellie—who was already nearly broke—found that her purse had gone missing, along with the last of her savings.

In the months and years to come, she would circle the globe, marry a millionaire and be widowed, take over his manufacturing empire, and become an influential businesswoman. But for now, Nellie Bly, who came to New York in search of "new worlds to conquer," was penniless. She was also too proud to give up. "Indeed," she wrote later, "I cannot say the thought ever presented itself to me, for I never in my life turned back from a course I had started upon."

Alone and robbed of her life savings in a city of more than a million people—a vast human stew into which hopeful and ambitious young women disappeared every day, never to be heard from again—Nellie rallied. "Energy rightly applied and directed," as she would later put it, "will accomplish anything."

She walked home, borrowed ten cents carfare from her landlady, and headed downtown to 31–32 Park Row, the offices of the *World*, the most successful and imitated newspaper in the country under the visionary

Left: The offices of the New York World *before 1890.*

leadership of its owner and publisher. Joseph Pulitzer had immigrated to America from Hungary at seventeen, and his rags-to-riches life story and populist approach must have appealed to a struggling upstart like Nellie, who was no stranger to obstacles. Often ill and always busy, the legendary publisher was unlikely to have been present himself that day, but the desire to prove her mettle and to belong (not to mention to earn the money she needed to survive and stay in New York) must have been intense. With its provocative and sometimes sensational reporting, its crusades and contests, its flashy headlines and lavish illustrations, and its direct appeal to immigrants and the working class, the *World* was Nellie's first-choice employer, and she was never one to aim low.

She "had to do a great deal of talking" to get past security and into the lobby, and no sooner had Nellie cleared the elevator than a clerk outside Colonel John Cockerill's office notified her that the editor in chief, who hired and supervised reporters, didn't take kindly to being disturbed. There was no point negotiating.

She parked herself in a chair in the outer office, refusing to budge, and took the opportunity to observe the *World*'s inner workings.

Segregated "male"/"female" classified ads in the Chicago Tribune, *1892.*

WORKING GIRLS BEWARE

Hundreds of trains entered the city nicknamed Gotham every day, many delivering single young women. Of these multitudes, some had never set foot in any city, much less one of the largest and loudest in the world, in search of their fortunes. "Never before in civilization," the urban reformer Jane Addams wrote a few years later, "have such numbers of young girls been suddenly released from the protections of the home and permitted to walk unattended upon city streets and to work under alien roofs; for the first time they are being prized more for their labor power than for their innocence, their tender beauty."

In New York and other cities, tender beauties arrived in droves to work in offices and factories, prey to those who would exploit them. On March 30, 1890, a bank official advertised in the help-wanted section of the *Chicago Tribune* to warn female stenographers of "our growing conviction that no thoroughly honorable businessman who is this side of dotage ever advertises for a lady stenographer who is a blonde, is good-looking, is quite alone in the city, or will transmit her photograph. All such advertisements upon their face bear the marks of vulgarity, nor do we regard it safe for any lady to answer such unseemly utterances."

As soon as she got the chance, Nellie herself advised caution in "Working Girls Beware," an article exposing a plot to rob needy female job seekers of their money.

The building would have hummed with activity and industry: anxious newsboys racing back and forth, trafficking cables from the paper's foreign correspondents; compositors setting copy into lead columns; giant cylinders spitting out spooled ribbons of printed newssheet; artists stooped in their curtained workshop, reconstructing crime scenes with steel-tipped pens; men piling mail-bags onto oily loading docks for delivery.

a very *good* idea it was—somewhere else. Maybe she casually trotted out the names of editors just interviewed for her article on women journalists. Whatever she said, it worked. Nellie soon found herself across the desk from the *World*'s imposing editor in chief.

A *printing mat, the* New York World.

Linotype compositors at work, the New York World.

In due course, Nellie started in on the clerk again. If the esteemed editor couldn't be persuaded to see her, she would be forced to take her idea—and

Infamous for his creative use of profanity and for the fact that he had once shot to death, under questionable circumstances, a St. Louis lawyer named Alonzo William Slayback, Colonel Cockerill didn't suffer fools. Nellie had already made his acquaintance during their interview for "Women Journalists" and knew not to waste his time.

She would sail to Europe and return in steerage, she proposed, getting a firsthand scoop on the filthy, overcrowded conditions many immigrants endured on the dangerous crossing to America. It was ambitious, but she knew she could pull it off. Her experiences writing about factory girls in Pittsburgh and reporting in Mexico had seasoned her.

Cockerill, who recognized talent when he saw it, must have seen some spark in Nellie. He fronted her twenty bucks to hold her services and agreed to talk her proposal over with the publisher.

In the end, Pulitzer shot the idea down. When Cockerill called Nellie back, he had something more local—if in the same spirit of reform—in mind, the sort of story the paper already excelled at. Would Miss Nellie Bly be able to get herself admitted into the insane asylum on Blackwell's Island to report on conditions there?

We can only imagine her state of mind as the editor's question hung in the air and the realities of day-to-day life in even a well-managed asylum dawned on her. Did she turn away . . . pause to think it through? What would she do instead? Admit defeat, turn tail, and return to Pittsburgh? Submit to a life of writing society gossip? Did Nellie feel that she had a choice? Or did the risks excite her?

When she looked her new editor in the eye and agreed, even the opportunistic Cockerill didn't express much faith in her chances of success. Her "chronic smile" worried him, for one thing; it was bound to give her away. "You can try," he said, and then, almost soothingly: "If you can do it, it's more than anyone would believe."

Vowing to "smile no more," Nellie demanded, "How will you get me out?"

"I don't know," he said. "Only get in."

Above: Colonel John A. Cockerill around 1895.

A SHADOW ON THE SUN

After a tour in the Union army cavalry, Joseph Pulitzer had wandered into New York, down on his luck, and walked into a hotel called French's for a shoeshine, only to be bounced out for sporting a shabby uniform. In a feat of poetic justice, the young man went west, made his fortune in law, politics, and journalism, and returned to set himself up in New York. He bought the ailing *New York World* newspaper in 1883 and promised, in an editorial, a "journal dedicated to the cause of the people," one that would "expose all fraud and sham" and "fight all public evils and abuses."

In the first three months, he doubled the paper's circulation.

Two years after Nellie's first visit to the *World*, Pulitzer bought French's and tore it to the ground. On the site of his former humiliation, across the street from (and casting into shadow) his staunch rival, Charles Dana's the *Sun*, Pulitzer would construct the city's tallest building to house his publishing empire.

Crowning the building was a great golden dome: when new immigrants approached the city of New York by sea, as Pulitzer had once done, his glimmering promise was their first experience of America.

His office at the tip-top of the building overlooked his adopted city,

Above: Joseph Pulitzer around 1900.

and on the walls of a massive Park Row newsroom packed with rolltop desks, placards reminded his writers:

**ACCURACY, ACCURACY, ACCURACY!
WHO? WHAT? WHERE? WHEN? HOW?
THE FACTS—THE COLOR—THE FACTS!**

Between the placards, huge windows revealed a city swarming with human life, its population growing at a breakneck pace as the newly invented elevator and expanding railway system spread the city's boundaries up and out. At the *World*'s peak in the 1890s, some million readers—a healthy segment of that population—began the day between its pages.

Newspaper Row around 1890: the World *building, topped by Joseph Pulitzer's shining dome, is visible on the left.*

3: strange
AMBITION

Who could tell but that the strain
of playing crazy and being shut up
with a crowd of mad people might
turn my own brain and I would never
get back.

Nellie had never spent time around the mentally ill and had no idea how the afflicted behaved. The only instruction Cockerill gave her was to use the name Nellie Brown so that, once in, she could be located. *How* she got in, convincing experienced doctors that she was insane, was entirely up to her.

"When evening came," she reported, "I began to practise the role in which I was to make my debut on the morrow."

Her first stop was the mirror.

"I had read of the doings of crazy people, how first of all they must have staring eyes, and so I opened mine as wide as possible and stared unblinkingly at my own reflection. I assure you the sight was not reassuring, even to myself, especially in the dead of night."

Between stare-downs, she read ghost stories by dim gaslight to maintain a sufficiently unnerved state of mind.

After what must have been a night of tossing and turning, she woke and performed her morning rituals—bathing, brushing her teeth, eating breakfast—"slowly and sadly," as if she might never know such ordinary pleasures again. She put on old clothing, a simple but dignified flannel dress and a black sailor's hat with a veil, thumbed through a directory, and made her way to the Temporary Home for Females, a boardinghouse on Second Avenue.

Posing with a dreamy, faraway look in her eyes, she rang the bell and was escorted in. She rented a thirty-cent shared room, registering as "Nellie Brown." She spent most of the day in a drab parlor where women sat staring into space or absently knitting, and where her restlessness— "the longest day I had ever lived!"— nourished her performance.

After a cheerless supper of beef, potatoes, coffee, and bread ("the repulsive form charity always assumes!" she would complain in her report), Nellie returned to her grim surveillance in the parlor. Though the doorbell rang nonstop with new arrivals, it was a "wretchedly lonely evening" spent in the dim gaslit parlor. She began to feel truly "fit" for the place she was "striving to reach."

Nellie went out of her way to avoid conversation, and when the assistant matron, Mrs. Stanard, approached to inquire, "Have you some sorrow or trouble?" she blurted out, "Yes, everything is

so sad" and then, in a dramatic whisper, motioning to her companions, "Why, they look horrible to me; just like crazy women. I am so afraid of them."

At bedtime, she acted too scared to sleep, sitting on the stairs and refusing to budge until the maid and a nurse inquired after her. The curious gathered to murmur. Nellie caught whispers of "Poor loon!" and "She will murder us all before morning." The woman she was supposed to bunk with announced that she would not stay "with that crazy woman for all the money of the Vanderbilts."

When nobody else would brave Nellie and her odd behavior, another guest at the boardinghouse, kind Mrs. Caine, volunteered to share her room.

While Nellie sat on
the edge of the bed
perfecting her blank
stare, the older woman
questioned her roommate
gently, noting how her eyes
"shone terribly brightly." Mrs.
Caine also helped calm
things later when screams
cut the night—those of a
woman having a "hideous
nightmare" about Nellie, it
turned out—working the house
into an uproar again. "She had
seen me, she said, rushing
at her with a knife in my
hand, with the intention
of killing her," Nellie wrote
later, taking an almost boast-
ful pride in her acting ability. But she
expressed guilt, too, throughout her
investigation, at having to de-
ceive good people like Mrs.
Caine: "It is only after one is
in trouble that one realizes
how little sympathy and kindness there are in the world."

Determined to stay up all night
(to appear even more gaunt
and unstable in the morning),
Nellie reflected on how certain
incidents are links in a chain of
"unchangeable fate." The "turned-
down pages" of her life were
"turned up" that night,
"and the past was
present."

As cockroaches
scurried over her
pillow, she recalled
old friends and enemies, joys
and heartaches; she wondered and
doubted, tossed and turned;
would she be able to pull
it off, "pass over the river
to the goal of my strange
ambition to become
eventually an in-
mate of the halls
inhabited by my
mentally wrecked
sisters"? She called this the
"greatest night of [her] existence," a night that put her
"face to face with 'self.'"

A CHANGE IN FORTUNES

Perhaps one of the events of "unchangeable fate" that Nellie had in mind that night in the Temporary Home for Females was the loss, at age six, of her beloved father.

Michael Cochran was an important man in Armstrong County, Pennsylvania. After buying property on the banks of Crooked Creek near his native Apollo, he opened a general store and modernized the village's four-story gristmill. In 1855, Pitts' Mills was renamed Cochran's Mills in his honor, and a five-year term of office as associate justice of Armstrong County earned him the honorary title "Judge."

When Elizabeth Jane (Pink) was born, her father already had ten other children with his first wife, Catherine Murphy, who died in 1857. He married Pink's mother, Mary Jane Cummings—a childless widow—a year later. Mary Jane gave birth to two children (Albert and Charles) before Pink, and two more (Catherine [or Kate] and Harry) after.

With the first generation of the judge's children grown and gone, and only Mary Jane's five living at home, he relocated his family back to his hometown, twenty-five miles from Pittsburgh. A mill town ringed in evergreens, Apollo revolved, like many small American towns of the time, around Main Street with its general store and drugstore. The town had no bank until 1871, but it had a blacksmith, a slaughterhouse, and a few taverns.

The judge built Mary Jane a grand two-and-a-half-story house on "Mansion Row" with plenty of land for the family horse, cow, and dogs, and parked a pleasure carriage out front.

But less than a year after settling his family into their graceful new home, two months after Pink's sixth birthday, the judge took sick and died.

The former associate justice, doting husband, and father of more than a dozen had never made a will.

He must have wanted security for his wife and young children, but with no legal instructions—and nine grown offspring waiting to claim a piece of his wealth—the judge's home and property were sold within a year of his death. Mary Jane kept the household furniture, a horse and carriage, the cow, one dog, and a small weekly allowance from the "widow's third" she was due under Pennsylvania law. While her children were at home, she would receive sixteen dollars a week and, after that, less.

It was a hard blow for a leading family.

Mary Jane rented a house a tenth of the size of the one on Mansion Row. It wasn't far away, but it might have been in another world.

The judge's untimely death proved to be just the beginning of a change in fortunes that would point young Pink on a path to her destiny. Over the next couple of years, Mary Jane sold the horse, carriage, and cow to carn income and, by 1873, was ready to make a desperate choice. Pink was nine when her mother married John Jackson Ford, who went by Jack. A veteran of both the Civil War and the 1850s Gold Rush, Jack Ford was also a nasty drunk. The family would live for five years in fear of his rages until, in 1878, Mary Jane braved shame and scandal to sue her children's abusive stepfather for divorce.

Background: Map of Apollo, Pennsylvania, 1896.

As morning seeped into the dingy rooms of the boardinghouse, Nellie began to rant about her missing belongings. Her trunks were gone, and she wanted them back. As her cries escalated, someone suggested that it might be prudent to involve the authorities, and when the assistant matron put on her bonnet, Nellie knew she was on her way. The stage was set.

Mrs. Stanard brought the police, and together they escorted her to Essex Market Police Court, a crowd of bedraggled children collecting behind, a ragged Greek chorus, making remarks. Passersby looked on with wide-eyed pity, and as they entered the building, Nellie began to worry.

To keep her foot in the door of the *Pittsburgh Dispatch* and earn freelance income, she had been sending George Madden the occasional New York City–based report (careful not to step on the toes of the *Dispatch*'s official New York correspondent, who wouldn't have taken kindly to the incursion). Only ten days earlier, she had met and questioned a resident police captain for one of these freelance articles, and "sure enough," when she walked in, "there was sturdy Captain McCullagh standing near the desk." Would he recognize her? She pulled her cap down low, shading her face as Mrs. Stanard explained her behavior.

Nellie's heart sank again as she was escorted through a milling crowd into the courtroom where her fate would be decided. Up behind his high desk, Judge Patrick Duffy had a kindly look about him. If he was *too* kind and compassionate, he might spoil her plans. Introduced as a woman "who doesn't know who she is or where she came from," Nellie picked up her refrain about the missing trunks, but the judge cut in cheerily that she looked like his sister. Anyone could see that she was "a good girl."

When no one could identify the good girl, however, a policeman offered: "Send her to the Island."

"Oh, don't," Mrs. Stanard protested. "She is a lady and it would kill her to be put on the Island."

Nellie "felt like shaking her."

"I am positive she is somebody's darling," the judge persisted, which made the crowd laugh and forced Nellie to cover her face with a handkerchief to hold back her own laughter.

But still, she worried. If someone recognized her, the game was up.

Perhaps noting her discomfort, and her assumed accent, Judge Duffy had her escorted to his private chambers and inquired if she might be from Cuba.

"Yes," Nellie replied with a smile, seizing the day—and a chance to use the Spanish she had picked up on assignment in Mexico two years earlier. "How did you know?"

"Oh, I knew it, my dear. Now, tell me where was it? In what part of Cuba?"

"On the hacienda," was her sly answer.

"Ah," said the judge, "on a farm. Do you remember Havana?"

"*Sí, señor.*"

Her real name was Nellie Moreno, she would later tell reporters, though she went by the English "Nellie Brown," but for now she complained to the sympathetic judge, "Everybody is asking me questions, and it makes my head worse."

Concluding that she might be drugged, Judge Duffy proposed a preliminary exam at Bellevue Hospital and, to Nellie's chagrin, called for reporters. A bit of publicity might help the court establish the pretty and cultured young lady's identity, he argued.

For her part, Nellie was far more concerned about having to fool reporters, whom she called "bright specimens of my craft," than she was about law enforcement officials or doctors. ❧

A FREE AMERICAN GIRL

Near the end of 1885, some nine months into her first job as a staff reporter, Nellie quit the *Pittsburgh Dispatch*, though she went on writing for the paper as a freelancer. She was twenty-one, restless, and bent on adventure.

She had overheard two of her mother's boarders, young railway workers, talking about Mexico. The country remained a mystery to most people north of the border, an exotic world apart, but if these men were right, it was, in fact, an easy train trip away.

Her racing mind kept her up all that night. The next day, Bly cornered George Madden and pressed him to assign her as *Dispatch* correspondent to Mexico. Not a chance, the editor cautioned. Too dangerous. But it was another good idea, one that would increase the *Dispatch*'s circulation, and Madden knew it. Nellie was persuasive, and he agreed to publish her articles.

By early 1886, she had enlisted her mother as chaperone (young ladies didn't voyage alone), traveling four days by train to disembark below the border with very little Spanish and the attitude of "a free American girl." Establishing a base in Mexico City, Nellie and her mother explored the countryside by train, shocking onlookers by defiantly carrying their own bags.

Nellie tracked down English-speaking contacts throughout Mexico and filed stories on everything from bullfights, pyramids, and floating gardens to the country's presidential history and courtship traditions. She discovered, with delight, an entire street devoted to coffin manufacturers. She tackled Mexican stereotypes native to the United States.

> Mexicans have never been represented correctly. Before leaving home I was repeatedly advised that a woman was not safe on the streets of Mexico . . . thieves and murderers awaited one at every corner. . . . There are murders committed here, but not half so frequently as in any American city. . . . Women—I am sorry to say it—are safer here than on our streets.

In the beginning, Nellie was charmed by Mexico and Mexico by her. Her regard for its citizens held, but her view of the country's government soured, and her frank criticisms (her *Dispatch* articles eventually worked their way south of the border) agitated Mexican officials, who threatened to arrest her for bending national censorship laws.

By June, shaken by jail threats, Nellie had headed home to Pittsburgh with her mother. Over the coming months, she turned in bold critiques of President Porfirio Díaz and corruption below the border, faulting Mexican newspapers for failing to publish "one word against the government," which she called, "the worst monarchy in existence."

Her articles on Mexico would later be collected in *Six Months in Mexico* (Nellie dedicated the book "To George A. Madden, managing editor of the *Pittsburg Dispatch*, in remembrance of his never-failing kindness"), but in time she ran out of material from her travels.

Madden hired her back on staff, but the reunion was short-lived.

After a few dull assignments, her restlessness reared its head again. One April day, without a word, she failed to come to work.

She did leave behind a note for her friend Erasmus Wilson, also known as Q.O., or the Quiet Observer. Nellie Bly was New York–bound.

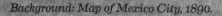
Background: Map of Mexico City, 1890.

4: you won't GET OUT in a HURRY

> And so, I passed my second medical expert. After this, I began to have a smaller regard for the ability of doctors than I ever had before.

Would Nellie be able to fool yet another clever expert? Judge Duffy stood by to see her off as the ambulance surgeon for Bellevue Hospital directed her to stick out her tongue. He looked "in a sagacious manner" and felt her pulse. How did the heart of an insane person beat? Nellie wondered, holding her breath for good measure. The expert shone a light in her eyes to observe her pupils, repeating the judge's speculation that belladonna or deadly nightshade poisoning—which can cause hallucinations and delirium—might underlie her condition, though Nellie insisted she had taken no drugs.

After affectionate good-byes from Judge Duffy, she traveled by ambulance to the "insane pavilion" at Bellevue Hospital. Chilled to the bone behind closed doors, she refused to remove her hat when a nurse asked her to.

"It will be a long time before you get out if you don't do as you are told," she was advised. Nellie asked for something warm to put on, and the nurse delivered a musty, moth-eaten shawl. When Nellie objected, the nurse said, "Well, some people would get along better if they were not so proud. . . . People on charity should not expect anything and should not complain."

Nellie kept her head covered with the shawl all day when possible, ostensibly against the cold but in fact to avoid being recognized. Visitors began to arrive, asking to see the missing girl, and for each she was instructed to lower her shawl, but no one recognized her.

Many were reporters: "Such a number of them!" The journalists who looked in were gentle and respectful as they questioned her but all "so bright and clever," Nellie wrote later. "I was terribly frightened they would see I was sane."

Later, in the kitchen, a maid named Mary whispered, "Have ye any pennies . . . they'll take them all from you anyway, dearie, so I might as well have them." Nellie also met another arguably sane inmate that day: Miss Anne Neville, a young chambermaid "sick from overwork." When the girl's health failed, her family had sent her to a Sisters' Home for treatment but were unable to pay her expenses, so they moved her to Bellevue instead. When Nellie asked, "Do you know only insane people are sent to this pavilion?" Anne replied that she did. But what could she do? The doctors wouldn't hear her.

After she repeated her story and explained again that she was from Cuba, the admitting doctor who questioned Nellie said, "Tell me, are you a woman of the town?"

After Nellie dignified this suggestion that she might be a prostitute, and "many more questions fully as useless," with a reply, the doctor declared her "positively demented." Miss Moreno was a hopeless case and needed to be sent "where someone will take care of her."

Yet another examiner, the head of Bellevue Hospital's insane pavilion, directed Nellie to stretch her arms, move her fingers, and open and close her eyes. Did she see faces on the wall? Did she hear voices? What did the voices say?

Bemused, Nellie told the doctor that she didn't listen, unless they happened to be talking about Nellie Brown.

"Softening of the brain," he murmured to a nurse. He would repeat the admitting physician's diagnosis to the *Herald*: "sheer delusion."

Nellie had fooled the doctors and would outwit her colleagues, too.

The next day, the *Evening Telegram* reported that the mystery woman was "undoubtedly insane."

The *Sun* ran her story, titled "Who Is This Insane Girl?" on the front page, describing her as a pretty but disoriented young lady with a mild air of cultivation. The baffled doctors, the paper offered, had never seen a case to rival it.

The *Times* called Nellie a "mysterious waif." Her confusion was heartbreaking, the reporter maintained, and she spoke in a plaintive whisper, repeating the same haunting refrain: "I can't remember."

When she left the exam room and the next patient entered, Nellie listened in as she was put to the same few tasks, asked the same few questions. Nothing much changed from interview to interview, and when Miss Tillie Mayard begged to know why she had been brought to this kind of hospital, the doctor answered, in surprise:

"'Have you just found out you are in an insane asylum?' . . .

"'Yes; my friends said they were sending me to a convalescent ward to be treated for nervous debility. . . . I want to get out of this place immediately.'

"'Well, you won't get out in a hurry,' he said, with a quick laugh.

"'If you know anything at all,' she responded, 'you should be able to tell that I am perfectly sane. Why don't you test me?'

"'We know all we want to on that score,' said the doctor," and, in Nellie's words, "left the poor girl condemned to an insane asylum, probably for life, without giving her one feeble chance to prove her sanity."

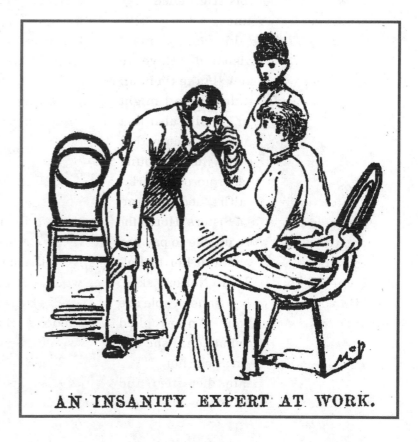

AN INSANITY EXPERT AT WORK.

THE ISLAND

Publishers and journalists saw it as their public duty to expose neglect and abuse at charitable and penal institutions. Such news stories were commonplace, but no one had attempted anything on the scale of Nellie's investigation. Among those who questioned conditions at Blackwell's were touring English author Charles Dickens, in his 1842 book *American Notes*, and author-editor Margaret Fuller for the *New-York Tribune*: "We saw, with pleasure," Fuller wrote, "tame pigeons walking about among the most violent of the insane, but we also saw two attendants with faces brutal and stolid. Such a charge is too delicate to be entrusted to any but excellent persons."

In fact, New York newspapers had been turning a spotlight on the institutions of Blackwell's Island all summer. The *World* published two editorials in July calling for investigation into "disgracefully overcrowded" conditions on Ward's Island—in the East River, just north of Blackwell's. Around the same time, two employees were indicted for manslaughter in the death of a "lunatic" there. The *Times* ran regular reports of alleged incidents on Blackwell's Island.

Known today as Roosevelt Island, the island is a narrow strip of land less than two miles long in the East River. Together with Ward's Island, it helped shape the city's history as home to prisons, charity hospitals, almshouses, workhouses, and what Nellie's editor, Colonel Cockerill, called "other cancer spots of modern Manhattan."

Looking back from the twenty-first century, it's hard to equate "modern" with 1887. But when Nellie left the *World* offices that day to hatch her plan, her adopted city was in the heat of explosive growth. Urban development and industrialization had people flooding in from around the country and the world, and a swelling population of convicts, the sick, the poor, and the insane marked the pains of that growth. New York City needed a place to warehouse these so-called undesirables.

In 1828, the city bought the island and built a jail and, less than a year later, a lunatic asylum to house inmates from Manhattan's Bellevue Hospital. When it opened in 1839 at the north end of the island, the asylum was the city's first publicly funded mental hospital and the first municipal mental hospital in the nation. A smallpox hospital followed in 1854, for quarantining victims and checking the spread of the disease.

With the East River forming what one historian called "a moat" around these fortresslike institutions, the citizens of Manhattan could sleep soundly at night. Some seven thousand failed specimens of humanity were held at bay and hidden in plain sight on Blackwell's.

But you needed an agency permit to board the round-trip ferry that circled from East Twenty-Sixth Street to the island twice a day, so only the committed or the condemned found it easy to get on (and it was never so easy to get off). The setting that made it convenient and discreet also made it harder to regulate and, when necessary, reform conditions of care for those inside. Isolating the doomed and dangerous on an island was a recipe for neglect.

The asylum, designed as a state-of-the-art facility, would carefully classify its inmates for treatment and keep the "noisy, destructive, and violent" separate from "idiots," "convalescents," and harmless "incurables." All would be housed humanely, without barricades or iron bars, and enjoy access to the outdoors. That was the goal. But the model didn't hold.

Though the lunatic asylum was split into three separate buildings—the Asylum, the Lodge, and the Retreat—in the end there was only enough funding for two residential wings, male and female, with dangerous or suicidal patients confined to the Lodge. And convicts from the neighboring penitentiary were put to work as attendants, leaving patients "abandoned," in one doctor's words, "to the tender mercies of thieves and prostitutes."

On Monday morning the patients received notice that they would depart for the island at one thirty. A nurse cut Nellie's fingernails to the quick while others speculated aloud that a lover had cast Nellie "forth on the world" and "wrecked" her brain. Reporters arrived all morning, but to her relief, Nellie was placed off-limits before any could question her. As the time for departure loomed, she grew more agitated, convinced that each new arrival would find her out.

She slipped Mary the kitchen maid a few pennies in passing, and a rough attendant saw Nellie and four other patients out to the ambulance and bolted the door behind.

When they reached the east-side pier, a crowd pushed in against the wagon, and a police presence was required to part them and allow Nellie and the other patients to step down and board the boat. They were escorted along the plank into a filthy, close cabin with a bunk that smelled

A female patient being transported from Bellevue Hospital to Blackwell's Island, 1896.

so bad Nellie had to hold her nose. A sick girl was unceremoniously set there, and they were guarded by two "fearful creatures," huge, coarse female attendants who spat tobacco juice on the floor "in a manner more skillful than charming."

When the boat docked across the East River, the patients were led up another plank to shore, where new guards herded them into yet another ambulance, clapped the springboard closed, making room for the officer and a mail carrier to jump aboard, and bumped past beautiful lawns toward what Nellie perceived in that moment as "a tomb of living horrors."

"What is this place?" she asked the man with thick fingers pinching the flesh of her arm.

"Blackwell's Island," he said, "an insane place, where you'll never get out of." ❧

LONELY ORPHAN GIRL

Forced to drop out of boarding school for financial reasons and weary from defeats beyond her control, the adolescent Pink must have welcomed her divorced mother's decision to move the family from Apollo—and a history marred by disgrace—to Pittsburgh, Pennsylvania, where her older sons had migrated in search of work.

Here was the fresh start the family needed.

After a country childhood, the steel capital of a greedily industrializing nation must have shocked sixteen-year-old Pink and her younger siblings. Teeming with more than 150,000 people, many of them veterans of the Civil War seeking work in its iron and steel mills, Pittsburgh was what one observer called "the blackest, dirtiest, grimiest city in the United States," the twelfth largest in the nation. Hundreds of factories, crowded within a few dozen square miles, cranked out not only iron and steel but copper, brass, cotton, and oil. Smoke poured from furnaces in all directions. Showers of soot rained down at odd moments, and the air stank of sulfur. Graphite flecks laced the breeze. The night sky often glowed fiery red, and if you strolled outdoors for long, your tongue took home the tang of metal.

Mary Jane settled her family in Allegheny City, an unincorporated suburb of Pittsburgh, in an industrial neighborhood of modest frame row houses, their backyards crisscrossed by railroad tracks. The family struggled to make ends meet, and Pink helped as she could. For the next four years she earned income as a housekeeper, kitchen girl, nanny, and tutor, though her heart and ambitions lived elsewhere.

Her even-less-educated brothers, meanwhile, landed respectable jobs as a clerk and manager of a rubber company. Three of her siblings married. The extended Cochran clan grew. Pink, who would never have children of her own, doted on her adoring nieces and nephews.

Mary Jane took in boarders to earn extra income. The neighborhoods her family lived in slowly improved, though Pink's prospects didn't.

What Pittsburgh lacked in clean air and polite charms, it made up for with newspapers. It was home to some ten dailies, including the *Pittsburgh Dispatch*. Erasmus Wilson— known as the Quiet Observer, Q.O. for short—published a popular column for the paper, and it was a Q.O. column that inspired Pink to a life in journalism, though "inspired" may not be the word, since it was outrage, not admiration, that roused her to write the letter to the editor that would launch her career.

PITTSBURGH DISPATCH BUILDING.

Wilson became a major influence on Pink, and a friend for life, but when his series opposing women in the workplace ran in the *Dispatch*, Pink was twenty and burdened with more practical responsibilities than many young men her age. Q.O.'s arguments must have boiled her ambitious blood.

Be an "angel," Wilson's column advised the ladies. Instead of laboring to succeed in business, stay home and make that place "a little paradise." A woman "outside her sphere" (and there was one word for it: home) was a "monstrosity." There was "no greater abnormality than a woman in breeches," his series asserted, unless it was "a man in petticoats."

Pink had spent the past four years of her life scraping by with her divorced mother in Allegheny row houses. She knew about the drive—the need—to earn her living outside the home, and said so. She signed her letter to the editor, "Lonely Orphan Girl."

At the time, Wilson's argument (though increasingly challenged in the socially turbulent years to come) wasn't unusual. But it took for granted the benefits of a traditional home, with a father or husband heading it up. Pink's choice of pen name was a reminder that not all women enjoyed such financial benefits.

Why did Pink cry orphan with her mother still alive? Losing the head of their household had left the Cochran family devastated and vulnerable. Her father's death spelled the end of safety and certainty, and for not the first time, Pink was writing from her own heart as much as from the heart of the issue, and her pen name was a direct emotional appeal.

Her story might have taken a different turn had the *Dispatch*'s managing editor, George Madden, not singled out Lonely Orphan Girl's letter and passed it along to Wilson, the Quiet Observer himself. "She isn't much for style," Madden told his star columnist, "but what she has to say she says right out." Lonely Orphan Girl's punctuation was laughable, the editor complained (and would go on complaining), but the girl had a voice, one that the *Dispatch*'s readers might like to hear.

Madden ran an ad in the January 17, 1885, edition of the paper inviting the anonymous writer to come forward and identify herself. "Lonely Orphan Girl" should "send her name and address to this office, merely as a guarantee of good faith," and the *Dispatch* would "confer a favor."

Pink skipped the formalities and turned up in person, a "shy little girl" out of breath from the stairs. Nervous if undaunted by the bustle of the newsroom, she asked an office boy to point out Madden. When the boy did, she declared, "Oh! Is it? I expected to see an old, cross man."

George Madden put Pink right at ease. He took her concerns seriously. Better yet, he invited her to weigh in on the topic of "the woman's sphere" herself. It was a challenge that changed Pink's life.

5: into the
MADHOUSE

I had some faith in my own ability
as an actress. . . . Could I pass a
week in the insane ward at Blackwell's
Island? I said I could and I would.
And I did.

She would be released in a few days. Nellie had faith in that. But her heart lurched anyway. She had been proclaimed insane "by four expert doctors and shut up behind the unmerciful bolts and bars of a madhouse." Anything must have seemed possible in that moment . . . even the idea that she might never cross the East River to freedom again.

The horizon soon revealed the two low stone buildings of the asylum. As she followed a narrow stairwell into the receiving room, she remembered the words of the guard who had gripped her arm so hard on the ambulance in, and his smug pronouncement chilled her.

Miss Tillie Mayard's entrance interview—in which the young patient had explained her recent physical illness and begged for more tests, with an argument Nellie called "as rational as any I ever heard"—was not the only cry for just diagnosis Nellie overheard in the asylum. She would meet other obviously sane patients in the coming days, including a young cook named Margaret who had been removed to the asylum after quarreling with coworkers. "How can they say I am insane merely because I allowed my temper to run away with me?" she pleaded. "Other people are not shut up for crazy when they get angry."

Nellie heard about a pretty young woman named Sarah Fishbaum who spoke little English: it was whispered that her husband had put her in the asylum "because she had a fondness for other men than himself."

It was clear that Mrs. Louise Schanz had not "one word of English," and when the doctor enlisted a nurse of German descent to interpret during Mrs. Schanz's interview, the nurse (embarrassed to be of immigrant stock herself, the eavesdropping Nellie deduced) all but refused, condemning the woman to the asylum without so much as giving her a chance to be understood.

Could such carelessness be excused, Nellie wondered as Mrs. Schanz pleaded in her native tongue, when it was possible to get an interpreter?

IF GIRLS WERE BOYS

The first article that "Lonely Orphan Girl" filed ran in the *Pittsburgh Dispatch* under the headline "The Girl Puzzle" on January 25, 1885. Imagine you're a hardworking, unmarried girl or widow, it urged readers. You're poor and ordinary, perhaps, without exceptional talent or beauty. You wear threadbare clothes and live in a single unheated room. If you have children, you often go hungry to keep them fed. You live in fear of the landlord turning you out into the wind and cold while selling your meager belongings out from under you. You aren't—can't be—above begging for work, any work, to secure your meager home and living.

Did society mean for these women to starve?

Pink urged the Haves to measure themselves against the Have Nots. Think about "what your last pug dog cost," she wrote. That "vast sum" might pay a family's doctor's bill or purchase new shoes for its children. How would the love and food you lavish on your favorite pet benefit families in need?

Sarah Fishbaum, Louise Schanz, and so many other immigrants—Nellie met a great many in the coming days—would have been better off as murderers, she thought. At least they would be tried before sentencing.

Listening in as these women were so carelessly condemned, Nellie felt her heart ache for them. She resolved to try by all means possible to benefit her "suffering sisters," to tell the world how they were shut away without due process.

Newsboys—and a lone newsgirl, nine-year-old Mary Malchade— picking up afternoon papers on Park Row, 1908.

"If girls were boys," wrote the twenty-year-old, "quickly it would be said: start them where they will, they can, if ambitious, win a name and fortune," advising, "gather up the real smart girls, pull them out of the mire, give them a shove up the ladder of life, and be amply repaid." If ambitious young men could start as errand or messenger boys, Pink proposed, working their way up to meaningful, well-paid jobs, why couldn't girls? No one thought twice about shutting a female worker up in an airless factory. Why not give her the chance to work in an office? Make her a conductor on the Pullman Palace car?

The *Dispatch* paid Pink for this first article, and for a second, "Mad Marriages," in which she tackled another topic of personal interest. With her mother's misfortunes raw in her mind, Pink boldly called for reform of Pennsylvania's divorce laws. Women needed options, she argued, when a husband's "dissolute habits"—alcoholism, laziness, financial negligence—threatened to make the home "wretched."

By the end of her own entrance interview, Nellie had determined to drop the act. "I made no attempt to keep up the assumed role of insanity." She talked and behaved normally from this point on. "Yet strange to say, the more sanely I talked and acted the crazier I was thought to be."

Her doctor spent most of his time flirting with the nurse on duty. "He gave the nurse more attention than he did me, and asked her six questions to every one of me. Then he wrote my fate in the book before him. I said, 'I am not sick and do not want to stay here. No one has a right to shut me up in this manner.' He took no notice."

Nellie's first supper in the asylum was a grab-and-snatch affair. The inmates had been made to wait an interminably long time in the unheated hallway outside the dining hall. The guards treated these cold, hungry, and agitated women—some laughing, crying, or "chattering foolish nonsense to invisible persons"—to the occasional shove, push, or slap on the ears while they waited, but when word came, they made a rush for a table lined with bowls of weak, pink tea, crude bread with rancid butter, and a few prunes, which were snatched up by those in the know.

"You must force the food down," Nellie's companion Annie Neville protested when Nellie refused, or "be sick, and who knows but with these surroundings you may go crazy. To have a good brain the stomach must be cared for." But Nellie couldn't take in anything but a bit of diluted, unsweetened tea.

That night, "to please the patients," she played a seriously out-of-tune piano in the sitting room while Miss Tillie Mayard sang (debuting with what Nellie

Hospital dining room, Blackwell's Island, around 1896.

An 1865 engraving depicting a "lunatic ball" at Blackwell's Island Asylum.

deemed a beautiful rendition of "Rock-a-bye Baby").

Music seems to have been the one acceptable diversion in the asylum. At one point during her stay, Nellie would be temporarily switched from Ward 6 to Ward 7, where a patient named Miss Mattie oversaw elaborate musical entertainments and dancing, making "the evenings pass very pleasantly. . . . Often the doctors come up and dance with the patients." In her exposé, Nellie ominously follows this reference with an account of patients hearing "a weak little cry in the basement. Every one seemed to notice it, and it was not long until we knew there was a baby down there. Yes, a baby. Think of it—a little, innocent babe born in such a chamber of horrors!"

At dinner her second night in the asylum, Nellie was famished and vowed to eat. Anything. The patients were made to stand out in the chilly hall again, this time for nearly forty-five minutes for bread, one cold, boiled potato, and a hunk of beef, "slightly spoiled." Deprived for safety's sake of knives and forks, the patients looked to Nellie "fairly savage as they took the tough beef in their fingers and pulled in opposition to their teeth." Women with tender teeth, or none, went hungry that night or subsisted, like Nellie, on a slice of bread.

Even without rancid butter, bread wasn't always a safe choice. One lunch was hard bread, "nothing but dried dough" in places and "a dirty black color." Nellie found a spider in hers, "so didn't eat." Again.

As a rule, asylum meals were "horrible messes" without salt or seasoning to speak of, though mustard and vinegar were freely used to give (or conceal) flavor. Sick inmates grew sicker over meals. Nellie once saw Miss Tillie Mayard "so suddenly overcome at a bite that she had to rush from the dining-room" and was scolded for doing so. The most afflicted patients might refuse to swallow their mess and were threatened with punishment. One young immigrant told Nellie that she "unceasingly prayed for death." The woman refused to eat for days, and one day, she was gone.

More than once, as staff meals were being prepared, Nellie glimpsed "beautiful white bread and nice meats," melons, grapes, and other fruits, which surely taunted the appetites of starving patients. Food, not surprisingly, was a favorite topic of discussion among the inmates, who outdid one another boasting of the

fanciful meals they would eat once they were citizens of the world again, once they were free.

That first night in the asylum, Nellie was led to a cold, wet bathroom and instructed to undress—every stitch—and submit to "one of the craziest women in the ward," who stood by the tub with a soiled-looking rag in her hand, "chuckling" in a manner that seemed to Nellie "fiendish." When Nellie opted to skip the bath, she was threatened with force, so she stood shivering while they stripped her of all but one garment. "I will not remove it," she insisted, but it was

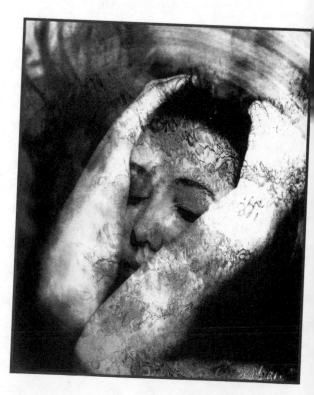

removed for her while patients gathered at the door to watch the struggle. Nellie hopped into the tub with "more energy than grace," begging that the onlookers be sent away, but she was told to shut up and dunked into the freezing water. The fiendish inmate scrubbed her all over with soap, rubbing it into her face and hair with force until she was "at last past seeing or speaking."

Feeling half-mad herself at this point, Nellie roared with laughter as they dressed her, dripping wet, in a short flannel slip stamped across the backside with large black letters: LUNATIC ASYLUM, B.I. H. 6.

"My teeth chattered and my limbs were goose-fleshed and blue with cold. Suddenly I got, one after the other, three buckets of water over my head—ice-cold water, too— into my eyes, my ears, my nose and my mouth. I think I experienced some of the sensations of a drowning person as they dragged me, gasping and shivering and quaking, from the tub. For once I did look insane."

"The letters," she wrote, "meant Blackwell's Island, Hall 6."

Tillie Mayard was up next, and Nellie winced to hear them plunge "that sick girl into a cold bath when it made me, who have never been ill, shake as if with ague." When Tillie begged for mercy—her head was sore from her recent medical emergency, she explained—the nurse warned, "Shut up, or you'll get it worse."

In the days to come Nellie determined that patients got one bath a week and it was the only time they saw soap. Women were bathed one after another in the same water until it was thick, at which time the tub was drained and refilled without a rinsing. Everyone used the same towel to dry off, and dresses on the ward were changed just once a month (unless a patient had a visitor, at which point a nurse hurried her into a fresh outfit to keep up appearances). Patients who couldn't or wouldn't see to their own hygiene had to be assisted by fellow patients.

Nellie would learn that the patients, in fact, *ran* the asylum—in the sense that they did most of the chores, from tending vast lawns and gardens to sewing clothing, doing laundry, making beds, and cleaning the nurses' rooms.

THE WORST GIRLS ON EARTH

As her first editor, George Madden, noted early on, Nellie wasn't "much for style." She was no wordsmith—and never let it stop her. Artful or not, her words pulsed with energy and confidence. They attracted and held readers' attention. Often they were a direct appeal, challenging readers to feel empathy for subjects and people outside their ordinary sphere of reference or imagination.

In an early article on the plight of Pittsburgh's poor working girls, Nellie chose to write about her subjects after hours. It would have been easy and natural to focus on the drudgery of the workday. Instead, by talking about what they did after work, like engaging in a vaguely scandalous activity called "man mashing"—the late nineteenth-century version of "hooking up" where young women went home with men they met on streetcars or in saloons—Nellie humanized anonymous women "tired of labor and longing for something new. Anything good or bad to break the monotony."

People opened up to Nellie ("I cannot go to places of amusement," one young worker lamented, "for want of clothes or money. . . . No one cares what becomes of me"). She wrote in a gossipy tone that pushed social boundaries, and her readers savored it. Put yourself in their shoes, Nellie seemed to say: "But for the poor working girl, without friends,

Background: Women working in a shoe factory around 1908.

without money and with the ceaseless monotony of hard work, who shall condemn and who shall defend?"

Her first big story for the *Dispatch* was a series on working conditions in eight Pittsburgh factories where women assembled everything from cigars to barbed wire. Many toiled twelve or more hours a day to earn a dollar.

For their trouble, female workers were often shamed or looked down on. "I had always been told factory girls were the worst girls on earth," one admitted, but you "can be a lady as well in a factory as in a parlor."

The series ran every Sunday for two months, with its own designed logo blazoned with the headline, "Our Workshop Girls: Women's Labor in Pittsburgh." It's hard to know what kind of impact Bly and her editor intended the series to have, but if she set out to write a probing chronicle of social ills, the work fell short. Nellie had the instincts to pitch a good story. She was already a disarming interviewer. But she hadn't yet refined the "undercover" or "stunt" reporting methods that would make her famous. With factory managers eager to make a good impression, and workers afraid to criticize and risk their jobs, Nellie's earnest report on factory life only grazed the surface.

Her open interviewing style gave intimate glimpses into the lives and emotions of female workers but only hinted at questionable conditions, child labor, or other flaws in a controversial system.

Was she frustrated with the end result? Was Madden, her first editor and mentor, disappointed?

Either way, this story was an important practice run for her influential asylum exposé.

After her bath that first night, Nellie was directed to sleep on a bed with a mattress "high in the centre and sloping on either side." Her wet hair soaked the pillow and the nurse refused to give her a nightgown to replace her damp slip, saying, "We have no such things in this institution. This is charity and you be thankful for what you get."

When Nellie objected that the city paid to keep up such institutions and intended the inmates to be treated kindly, the nurse retorted, "Well, you don't need to expect any kindness here, for you won't get it."

Nellie slept that night on a sheet over an oilcloth, covered by a black wool blanket that was too short. Every time she pulled it up to warm her shoulders, her feet stuck out in the cold, and vice versa. Throughout the night, nurses in striped dresses, white aprons, and caps with keys dangling on cords at their waists came noisily in and out shining lanterns in her face.

Later she would be forced to take medication—it "smelt like laudanum and it was a horrible dose"—when a nurse noticed that she was lying awake. Threatened with an injection if she didn't swallow, Nellie obeyed, but the moment the nurse went out, she put a finger down her throat to bring it back up. "They inject so much morphine and chloral that the patients are made crazy. I have seen [inmates] wild for water from the effect of the drugs and the nurses refuse it to them. I have heard women beg for a whole night for one drop."

Exhausted though she was that first night, Nellie found herself up most of it worrying about fire. Every door in the asylum seemed to lock separately, and the windows were heavily barred. In her building alone there were some three hundred women, with between one and ten to a room. Would guards or nurses take the time to release these prisoners in an emergency, or would the inmates "roast to death" behind locked doors? When she later expressed this concern to a doctor, he shrugged it off: "What can I do?" ❧

A HUMILIATING ORDEAL

In a biographical sketch in the *World*, Nellie credited her knack for story-telling to sleepless nights. She spent the wee hours of her childhood "weaving tales," she claimed, and "creating heroes and heroines." But her insomnia had a dark side, too: "So active was the child's brain and so strongly her faculties eluded sleep that her condition became alarming and she had to be placed under care of physicians."

After her father's untimely death, Pink felt increasingly called to keep her mother and siblings safe and provided for. Somebody had to, but such intentions—to a child without the power to act on them—were a recipe for restlessness and deepest worry, the food of sleepless nights.

Mary Jane knew that in the 1880s life without the support of a husband or father was hard enough for a grown woman, especially a twice-widowed forty-three-year-old raising five children on a shoestring in a small town. Her disastrous remarriage to Jack Ford was less about convenience than necessity, though in the end it proved unbearable. After the divorce, Pink's mother shed the name Ford—becoming "the widow Cochran" again—and set about rubbing the humiliating ordeal off the family record.

That same ordeal, though, fanned Pink's little flame of devotion and responsibility into a bonfire. Even with two older brothers, she now saw it as her duty to shelter and defend her mother. A life of committed service to a husband and family was clearly no guarantee of success or security. Her exhausted parent may have been in the market for a champion, but the takeaway, for Pink, was that a woman must do for herself.

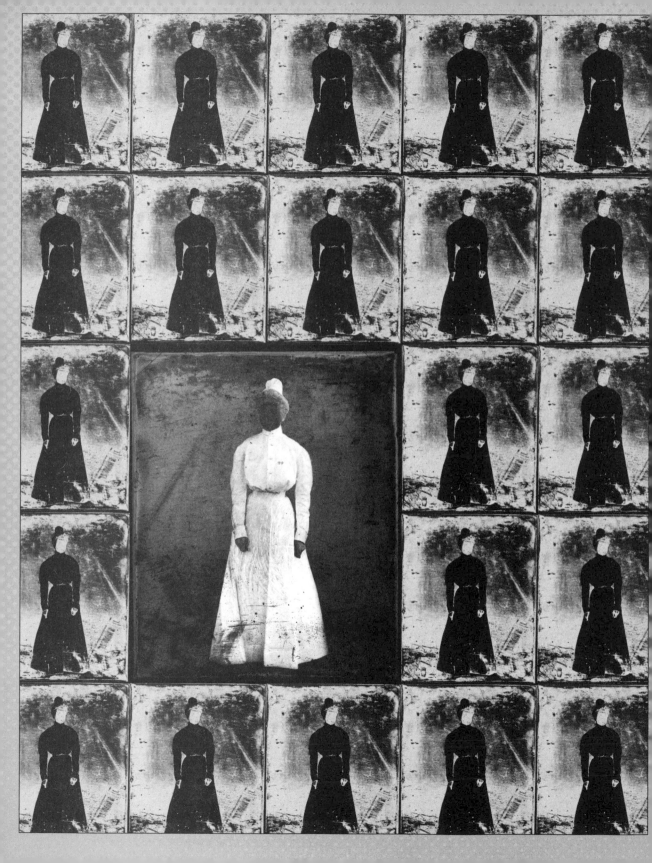

6: SHE who enters HERE

> What, excepting torture, would produce insanity quicker than this treatment?

The next morning Nellie woke aching all over from a night in wet clothes. A nurse threw open her window and roughly removed her slip. She handed Nellie a cheap calico dress with a stain on it and led her back to the bath hall where the forty-five patients of Hall 6—a few with "dangerous eruptions all over their faces"—shared two towels among them. Nellie washed up at the faucet and used her underskirt to dry her face and hands. All forty-five had their hair combed by "one patient, two nurses, and six combs," wrote Nellie. "Oh, that combing!" Tangled and damp from the night before, her matted locks were "pulled and jerked" as her complaints went unheard. She gritted her teeth and endured.

From there, the day seemed to go on forever.

After completing numerous household chores, patients put on identical shawls and "comical" white straw hats—"such as bathers wear at Coney Island"—and were herded outdoors for a walk. Forming lines as far as the eye could see and guarded by nurses, the procession marched slowly around beautiful lawns tended by capable patients. They were not allowed on the grass, and at least once Nellie saw a patient lift an acorn or a bright leaf from the path, only to be told to put it down.

The walkers were a teeming mass of "old, gray-haired women talking aimlessly to space," women dragged along in straitjackets, women chattering to themselves and screaming, women crying, singing, or just staring blankly ahead. They were, Nellie observed, crippled, blind, young, old, homely, and pretty—"one senseless mass of humanity. No fate could be worse."

One especially dirty and raucous group passed by rigged up to a strange contraption. Each wore a wide leather belt locked around her waist and attached to a heavy iron cart by a long rope. These were violent patients from the Lodge, too

dangerous to walk on their own. A few years later, in his landmark 1889 book, *How the Other Half Lives*, "muckraking" journalist, photographer, and social reformer Jacob Riis described the same scene:

> *A file of women in the asylum dress of dull gray, hitched to a queer little wagon that, with its gaudy adornments, suggests a cross between a baby-carriage and a circus-chariot. One crazy woman is strapped in the seat; forty tug at the rope to which they*

An 1834 engraving of Blackwell's Island Asylum.

An 1866 engraving of the Retreat and Yard at Blackwell's Asylum.

are securely bound. This is the "chain-gang," so called once in scoffing ignorance of the humane purpose the con-trivance serves. These are the patients afflicted with suicidal mania, who cannot be trusted at large for a moment with the river in sight.

Nellie later heard dreadful stories from women who had, at one time, walked "on the rope." The Lodge, home to these particular patients, was no-toriously dirty, and the stench in summer brought swarming flies. One apparently sane former inmate of the Lodge told of a vicious beating that broke two of her ribs. She also reported being pulled around by the hair, held under water, and choked while a nurse stationed quiet patients as "watch" near the door to warn of approaching doctors. No one dared speak up about such treatment, the woman confided in Nellie, for fear of retribution.

"While I was there," the woman said, "a pretty young girl was brought in. She had been sick, and she fought against being put in that dirty place. One night the nurses took her and, af-ter beating her, they held her naked in a cold bath, then they threw her on her bed. Come morning she was dead. The doctors said she died of convulsions and that was all that was done about it."

During that first walk around the grounds, Nellie spotted a low pavil-ion with a motto emblazoned on the wall:

WHILE I LIVE I HOPE

The absurdity hit her hard. "I would have liked to put above the gates that open to the asylum:

HE WHO ENTERS
HERE LEAVETH
HOPE BEHIND"

But the worst hours were yet to come. After the morning promenade, patients were made to sit for hours on hard benches without any way to occupy or divert themselves. Those in the "sitting-hall" who tried to talk were ordered to shut up. Those who slumped or shifted or stood to work out the stiffness were told to sit up straight, keep still, or sit down.

When the superintendent of the asylum passed through and no one made a move to complain, Nellie asked why. Because they didn't want a beat-ing, of course.

BETWEEN THE BARS

The media kept its eye on the island between 1839 and 1895. Early features focused on the lunatic asylum's colorful inmates. This profile of a patient known as Mrs. Buchanan was published in *Harper's Weekly* some twenty years before Nellie set foot on the island:

> She is one of the incurables—a poor old lady—Scotch I imagine—who has been an inmate of the lunatic asylum for years. Her delusion has been described in the papers. She believes she is the wife of the President and discharges her conjugal duties with such success that she bears a large family to the President. Strange to say, the offspring of her lofty amours are invariably cats. I had the honor of stroking the back of President Buchanan's eldest son. . . .

The author, a former patient, admitted that Blackwell's had "no very good name" but managed to praise the picture-perfect setting with its flower gardens, willows, and pond. "The aspect of nature can not be too highly estimated in its effects upon the better class of patients," he wrote. It "helps them to relieve their minds of the fancies which oppress them."

By mid-century, though, the tone of media reports changed. Most, like the 1879 *Times* article "Tormenting the Insane," focused on alarming cases of neglect, abuse, and false confinement.

By Nellie's day, Blackwell's natural landscape no longer afforded much relief. As she observed, patients were barred from any real contact with it on their joyless strolls around the building. She described, too, the peculiar sensation of being so near and yet so far from the workings of the wider world:

> In the upper halls a good view is obtained of the passing
> boats and New York. Often I tried to picture to myself as I
> looked out between the bars to the lights faintly glimmering
> in the city, what my feelings would be if I had no one to
> obtain my release. I have watched patients stand and gaze
> longingly toward the city they in all likelihood will never
> enter again. It means liberty and life; it seems so near.

In a 1910 *Times* article, the warden of the neighboring penitentiary called the place "as pleasant as the Thousand Islands." The convicts, he said, worked in "big airy rooms through which cool breezes sweep," with views of "the yachts of millionaires" gliding past.

On the contrary, the busy to-ing and fro-ing of river traffic must have been a constant reminder of all they had lost. Every now and then prisoners made a break for it, as in 1853 when "12 nude men swam for freedom and were spotted coming out of the water at what is now Long Island City."

A couple of years after Nellie's visit, Jacob Riis called the asylum a place where "the light of hope and reason have gone out together":

> The shuffling of many feet on the macadamized roads
> heralds the approach of a host of women, hundreds upon
> hundreds—beyond the turn in the road they still keep
> coming, marching with the faltering step, the unseeing
> look and the incessant, senseless chatter that betrays the
> darkened mind. The lunatic women of the Blackwell's Island
> Asylum are taking their afternoon walk.

Blackwell's might house 1,700 women on any given day, but Riis noted "a constant ominous increase in . . . helpless unfortunates . . . thrown on the city's charities" and blamed the rise on the pressures of modern life but, above all, on poverty. Most of the inmates, not surprisingly, were poor. Most would never leave.

*Here is a class of women sent
to be cured? I would like the
expert physicians . . . to take
a perfectly sane and healthy
woman, shut her up and make
her sit from 6 A.M. until 8 P.M.
on straight-back benches, do
not allow her to talk or move
during these hours, give her
no reading and let her know
nothing of the world or its doings, give her bad food and
harsh treatment, and see how
long it will take to make her
insane. Two months would
make her a mental and physical wreck.*

Many patients reported cruel treatment at the hands of the nurses, or said they had witnessed it. One patient told of a blind woman who had begged for a shawl against the cold. When she tried to feel her way out of the room to find one, she was jerked back to the bench or taunted while she bumped into walls. One nurse ran cold hands over her face and under the fabric of her dress, and together with other nurses "laughed savagely" at her cries. When the same old woman tried to remove a pair of painful shoes, seven attendants descended on her to force them back on.

A woman who thought she had spotted her husband arriving, and who left the line in her excitement to meet him, was sent to a building ironically called "The Retreat" for punishment. When she cried, a nurse beat her with a broom handle, injuring her internally. At other times, nurses tied a twisted sheet around her neck, dunked her in cold water, knocked her head against the floor, and pulled out hunks of her hair by the roots. "Here Mrs. Cotter showed me proofs of her story," Nellie wrote, "the dent in the back of her head and the bare spots where the hair had been taken out by the handful."

Nellie herself often heard nurses and attendants "make ugly remarks and threats" and saw them "twist the fingers and slap the faces of the unruly patients." She was present when nurses ruthlessly teased a mentally challenged patient who happened to be sensitive about her age. When the woman waxed hysterical, they "pounced on her and slapped her face and knocked her head in a lively fashion. This made the poor creature cry the more, and so they dragged her into a closet and choked her. Yes, actually choked her. I plainly saw the marks of their fingers on her throat."

The nurses never addressed asylum inmates "except to scold or yell at them, unless it was to tease them," Nellie wrote, and "spent much of their time gossiping" about doctors and other nurses and using profane language. Attendants seemed to enjoy "exciting the violent patients to do their worst." And the doctors? There were sixteen on the island at the time, Nellie wrote, and "I have never seen them pay any attention to the patients. How can a doctor judge a woman's sanity by merely bidding her good morning and refusing to hear her pleas for release?"

"I have described my first day," she pronounced, and "my other nine were exactly the same."

Apart from rhapsodizing about what food they would eat when they made it back across the river, patients had little to entertain or engage them beyond "waiting enthusiastically for new unfortunates to be added to our ranks," at which point patients gathered around in sympathetic greeting, "anxious to show them little marks of attention." Hall 6 was the receiving hall, so its residents had first dibs on all newcomers.

Letters arrived but rarely. Nellie saw just one handed to a patient while she was there, and "it awakened a big interest. Every patient seemed thirsty for a word from the world, and crowded around asking 'hundreds of questions.'"

But one day in the midst of deadening routine, she was summoned to the sitting room. ✐

Woman inmates relegated to benches in the Ohio Insane Asylum more than half a century after Nellie Bly's exposé.

THE USUAL DUTIES

Why was Nellie willing to pose as a patient and risk her well-being for a story? She was motivated by the urge to do good, certainly. But it may be that, for an ambitious journalist, the benefits outweighed the risks.

On the heels of her Pittsburgh series on factory girls, Nellie interviewed clerks and servants. She proposed that poor girls needed and deserved a sanctuary to parallel the Young Men's Christian Association (YMCA) to "offer and give assistance." Too "impatient to work along at the usual duties assigned women on newspapers," she did her best to avoid being relegated to the women's pages, but time and again she found herself reporting on hair care, shoes, and flower shows anyway.

What was she up against? Of the roughly twelve thousand journalists in America in 1880, fewer than three hundred were women. Newsrooms back then, thick with cigar smoke, were male habitats. Reporters slugged from flasks, spit tobacco, reveled in profanity, and in general did what respectable men of the day believed they couldn't do at home or in public for fear of offending delicate female sensibilities.

The average reporter started as an office boy, running errands, sweeping floors, delivering copy, and enduring a hail of curse words from his superiors. It was a rough education, but the initiate saw firsthand what editors wanted from their reporters; he learned how stories were written and rewritten; and one day, he got his chance to file stories of his own.

People felt that young women like Nellie—however smart or strong—must be sheltered from such rude rites of passage. The idea that they could withstand the rigors of writing hard news was preposterous. City newsmen traveled alone at night into tenements and morgues, gambling dens and male-only dinner clubs. They rubbed elbows with criminals and cops. They witnessed riots, strikes, and fires. It was dirty work.

It was important work, too. The press was nicknamed the Fourth

Estate, right up there with judicial, legislative, and executive—the three branches of government defined by the Constitution. But with no US women's union or press club until 1889, "girl" reporters took their chances, often earning far less than men (some weren't paid at all, except "in compliments," as one writer put it).

Political reporter Jane Grey Swisshelm, the first woman journalist to watch Senate proceedings from a seat in the gallery, in 1850, lamented:

> They plough, harrow, reap, dig, make hay, rake, bind grain, thrash, chop wood, milk, churn, do anything that is hard work, physical labor, and who says anything against it? But let one presume to use her mental powers—let her aspire to turn editor, public speaker, doctor, lawyer—take up any profession or avocation which is deemed honorable and requires talent, and O! bring cologne, get a cambric kerchief and feather fan, unloose his corsets and take off his cravat! What a fainting fit Mr. Propriety has taken! Just to think that "one of the dear creatures"—the heavenly angels—should forsake the sphere— the woman's sphere—to mix with the wicked strife of this wicked world!

But newspapers are a business. While not many women wrote for them, plenty read them. More and more, publishers were meeting that consumer demand by assigning a slice of the paper to their female audience.

In these dedicated women's pages, the "fairer" sex found recipes and household tips. She found sentimental poems and reviews of romantic novels. She learned why women were afraid of mice, how to seat guests at a formal dinner, and what certain high-profile debutantes had worn to the latest ball. One reporter confessed that life, for society writers like her, was "one long-drawn-out five o'clock tea of somebody else."

Many women journalists found themselves mailing in quaint articles and struggling with boredom, frustration, and futility as their talents wilted in the confines of rigid subject matter.

BEHIND ASYLUM BARS

—※✧※—

The Mystery of the Unknown Insane Girl

—※—

REMARKABLE STORY OF THE SUCCESSFUL IMPERSONATION OF INSANITY

—※—

How Nellie Brown Deceived Judges, Reporters and Medical Experts

—※—

SHE TELLS HER STORY OF HOW SHE PASSED AT BELLEVUE HOSPITAL

—※—

Studying the Role of Insanity Before Her Mirror and Practising It at the Temporary Home for Women—Arrested and Brought Before Judge Duffy—He Declares She Is Some Mother's Darling and Resembles His Sister—Committed to the Care of the Physicians for the Insane at Bellevue—Experts Declare Her Demented—Harsh Treatment of the Insane at Bellevue—"Charity Patients Should Not Complain"—Vivid Pictures of Hospital Life—How Our Esteemed Contemporaries Have Followed a False Trail—Some Needed Light Afforded Them—Chapters of Absorbing Interest in the Experience of a Feminine "Amateur Casual."

7: after an
ITEM

> The insane asylum on Blackwell's Island is a human rat-trap. It is easy to get in but once there it is impossible to get out.

Stepping into the receiving room of Ward 6 in the guise of a madwoman, Nellie found herself face-to-face with a visitor ostensibly seeking a missing loved one. In fact, the man was a reporter, sent to get a gander of the mystery patient. Nellie knew him, and he was clearly shocked to discover her there, but she managed to whisper in a choked voice, "Don't give me away."

Banking on it, she turned to the attendant: "No. I do not know this man."

"Do you know her?" the visitor was asked.

"No, this is not the young lady I came in search of."

"It's all right," Nellie reassured him in the split second she had to explain. "I'm after an item. Keep still."

Luckily for her, and many others, he did.

Nellie had originally intended to "get violent" in order to be sent to the wards at the Lodge and Retreat, but once she had relevant testimony from sane former residents, she decided not to risk her health "and hair."

Her fellow arrival, Miss Tillie Mayard, had already suffered a swift decline. "I talked with her daily," Nellie wrote, "and I grieved to find her grow worse so rapidly." The young woman was always cold and had stopped eating. She "sang in order to try to maintain her memory, but at last the nurse made her stop it." It became clear that Tillie was lapsing into delusion, convinced that the visitors who came inquiring after Nellie were in fact her own visitors, her own friends, and that Nellie was somehow deceiving or detaining them. She wouldn't be reasoned with, and to ease the stress of her companion, Nellie now kept her distance.

"You have no right to keep sane people here," she again complained to the medical staff. "I am sane, have always been so, and I must insist on a thorough examination or be released. Several of the women here are also sane. Why can't they be free?"

"They are insane," came the refrain, "and suffering from delusions."

To her mounting horror, it became obvious that without help from her employer, Nellie might never escape the asylum. Her editor had proposed that a week inside would be enough, but after seven days and not a word from outside, a panicked Nellie wondered if rescue would come at all.

At last on October 4, her tenth day in the asylum, the *World* sent an attorney. Nellie Moreno, aka Brown, would be cared for by friends in the city, he proposed. Cartoonist Walt McDougall, who would soon illustrate many

of Nellie's *World* articles, accompanied the lawyer that day and years later reflected how an agitated crowd of female patients had circled him in the courtyard. "The way the mob rushed me," he said, "one would have thought I was the first train out after a subway hold-up."

Nellie was summoned for release during the morning walkabout, while assisting another patient who had fainted.

"I had looked forward so eagerly to leaving the horrible place yet when my release came . . . there was a certain pain in leaving. . . . For ten days I had been one of them. . . . It seemed intensely selfish to leave them to their sufferings."

After sad good-byes, Nellie crossed the East River "with pleasure and regret . . . that I could not have brought with me some of the unfortunate women who lived and suffered with me, and who, I am convinced, are just as sane as I was and am now myself."

Her two-part series debuted in the *World* the following week on October 9, 1887, with "Behind Asylum Bars," and in two weeks' time Nellie Bly was a sensation. The public couldn't get enough of her vivid and frightening tale of madness and misdoings, one that exposed not only Blackwell's medical and professional staff but her own colleagues, who had been just as duped by her exploits.

How had Joseph Pulitzer's young upstart managed not only to pass herself off as insane but to fool any number of seasoned professionals: doctors, nurses, administrators, judges and policemen, and, yes, fellow journalists?

The *World's* archrival, the *Sun*, responded by energetically deflecting attention with the headline: "PLAYING A MADWOMAN: Nellie Bly Too Sharp for the Island Doctors."

Her mission to benefit her "suffering sisters," though, wasn't yet complete. Near the end of October, Nellie was summoned before the grand jury. Intimidated at first, she "found the jurors to be gentlemen" and did not "tremble before their twenty-three august presences." The jury invited her to inspect the island with them, though Blackwell's was notified approximately an hour before the investigators arrived (they were tipped off, Nellie learned, while the jury stopped to examine the insane pavilion at Bellevue).

For Nellie, it was a very different voyage across the river. "We went on a clean new boat. The one I had traveled in they said was laid up for repairs."

When they arrived, Superintendent Dent told Nellie that in the wake of her article, he had "found a nurse at the Retreat who had watches set for our approach, just as you stated. She was dismissed."

The kitchen was now immaculate, with two barrels of salt open and strategically placed near the door. The bread was "beautifully white" and "wholly not" the bread patients had been given to eat while Nellie was in residence. Beds had been upgraded. Worn buckets had been replaced with shiny new basins.

But what had become of the patients, the many women Nellie had deemed sane and who were being held against their wills? Miss Anne Neville was called in, shaking with fear at the sight of so many male strangers and looking worse for wear. She confirmed that conditions had been grim but: "Strange to say ever since Miss Brown has been taken away everything is different. The nurses are very kind and we are given plenty to wear. The doctors come to see us often and the food is greatly improved."

The majority of the patients named or referenced in Nellie's exposé were nowhere in evidence. They had been removed—discharged, according to administrators, detained for health care, or transferred. The existence of one Mexican inmate was denied altogether, while a Frenchwoman Nellie had deemed "a great, healthy woman" was apparently "dying of paralysis, and we couldn't see her."

"If I was wrong in my judgment of these patients' sanity," Nellie wrote beseechingly, "why was all this done?"

She did manage to get a glimpse of Tillie Mayard, who "had changed so much for the worse that I shuddered when I looked at her."

On the face of things, the asylum was running just fine, and Nellie worried that her efforts to demonstrate otherwise might prove in vain. But in the end the jury advised the court to support the changes she proposed.

"I have one consolation for my work," she wrote, "on the strength of my story the committee of appropri-ation provides $1,000,000 more than was ever before given, for the benefit of the insane." In particular, $50,000 was budgeted for the asylum at Black-well's. Consensus to increase funding to beleaguered city institutions had been growing for a long time, but Nel-lie's bold intervention surely moved things along.

Her fame and acclaim soon spilled across New York borders. Newspapers all over North America demanded to know how so many experts could be taken in by a girl with no particu-lar training and, more troubling still, how it was that so many were "sent to asylums on the certificates of doctors who were in collusion with relatives

ROOSEVELT ISLAND

Despite reforms, the image of Blackwell's as "human rat-trap" hung on, and in 1894—seven years after Nellie's exposé—the New York City Lunatic Asylum on Blackwell's Island closed its doors forever. Today, only a domed octagonal building, the centerpiece of the institu-tion in Nellie's day, remains. In 1921, the island was renamed Welfare Island, another stab at undoing years of scandal and bad publicity. The interested in having them put out of the way."

Two months later, Nellie's articles were published together in book form—along with some filler—as *Ten Days in a Mad-House*. Her knack for placing herself front and center in her stories hooked readers, and her fan base grew along with the *World's* circulation numbers.

In a letter to her Pittsburgh friend and mentor signed—per custom with Erasmus Wilson—"Your naughty kid, Nellie Bly," Nellie bragged that she was no longer a nobody. She now held her own among mostly male colleagues at the *World*, and "no one in the office, but Col. Cockerill dare say a word to me. Somehow they treat me as if I was a pretty big girl." ❧

Cover of Bly's Ten Days in a Mad-House, *1887.*

Roosevelt Island, 2015.

penitentiary would soon follow the asylum's lead. Its inmates were relocated to a new jail on Rikers Island. Blackwell's is no longer a place to hide the city's difficult and doomed. Known today as Roosevelt Island, it's a developing residential area and the projected home of an ambitious graduate school for technology at Cornell University.

THE FIN DE SIÈCLE NEWSPAPER PROPRIETOR.

HE COMBINES HIGH-SOUNDING PROFESSIONS AND HIGH-SPICED SENSATIONS, AND REAPS A GOLDEN PROFIT THEREBY.

8: STUNTS and more STUNTS

Nellie's daring earned her a full-time job at the *World* and her own byline, quite an achievement at a time when most newspaper reports ran anonymously, that is, without crediting the author. Her stories became so popular that "by Nellie Bly" wasn't always flashy enough, and her name was worked right into bold headlines. Articles like "Nellie Bly on the Wing," "Nellie Bly as a Mesmerist," and "Nellie Bly as a Prisoner" inspired a loyal readership with some two hundred letters a week pouring in for her at the *World*, a few bearing threats, others marriage offers.

When an interviewer asked Joseph Pulitzer to comment on his bright new reporter, the publisher characterized Nellie as "plucky," a term that stuck.

She was kept busy with new stunts, passing herself off as a maid for an exposé of employment agencies and as an unmarried mother for a piece on a bogus agency "selling" unwanted babies. She got herself hired in a paper box factory where girls slaved all day for next to nothing in an airless room stinking of glue. She played a naïve pedestrian to entrap a man notorious for circling Central Park in his carriage to meet and exploit innocent girls. And she

Left: In this 1894 satirical cartoon, Joseph Pulitzer and his imitators reap profits by publishing sensational news.

forced the illustrious "Lobby King" of Albany, Edward R. Phelps, from his "throne" by pretending to be the wife of a patent salesman who wanted to kill a bill due for consideration by an Assembly committee. Phelps made it clear that he could buy off committee members in a jiffy for as little as a thousand dollar donation from Nellie's patent salesman husband. He even went so far as to make a pencil mark by the name of each man he would convince to change his "yes" vote to "no." When Nellie exposed the lobbyist's corruption, he was driven out of Albany in days.

"Nothing was too strenuous nor too perilous for her if it promised results," her colleague Walt McDougall said. "She was more than once held back from a too dangerous venture."

Nellie Bly was a star at one of the nation's most influential and innovative newspapers, and she was barely twenty-five years old. At last, she had enough money to bring her beloved mother, Mary Jane, to the city to live with her. They were a long way

NEVER HAVING FAILED

In early 1889, Nellie traveled to Perkins School for the Blind near Boston to interview a remarkable woman. Struck deaf and blind by fever as a child, Laura Dewey Bridgman had learned to speak with her fingers and, even more miraculously, to read and write, becoming a sort of girl wonder of the day. The visiting English writer Charles Dickens had interviewed Bridgman for his travelogue, *American Notes*, and his profile led Pink back for a second look at the woman she called the "*bête noire*" of her childhood.

Why would young Pink reduce an accomplished deaf, mute, and blind girl to the status of a hated nemesis?

Because whenever Nellie dared utter the words, "I can't," her mother trotted out Laura Dewey Bridgman as inspiration and example. If she can from their Pennsylvania home and gradually moved nearer downtown. Nellie changed her hair and made the acquaintance of fashionable dressmakers. She and Mary Jane began to take in shows and enjoy the many social delights of the city.

Imitation may be the sincerest form of flattery, but it would soon have—and keep—Nellie on her toes.

A strategy of Joseph Pulitzer's crusading "New Journalism" had long been to send his writers out in disguise to get the scoop on crime, exploitation, and scandal, but those writers had always been men. Nellie changed the game. Her highly successful asylum story launched the era of "girl" stunt reporters. Other women journalists soon saw the appeal of a reporting style that could get them off the dreary society beat, and Nellie's publisher saw an opportunity in his popular new star.

Laura Dewey Bridgman, Nellie Bly's childhood "bête noire," around 1855.

do it, with all her disadvantages, Mary Jane suggested, what's your excuse?

"I don't think it had the desired effect," Pink complained, "to shame little girls into doing that for which they had no inclination." Her mother's stab at character building had only made the child determined to "enjoy to the utmost those privileges of sight and speech and hearing of which [Bridgman] was deprived."

But Pink would one day reward Mary Jane's efforts, and a mother's faith in her willful daughter: "Never having failed," the famous journalist told her fans, "I could not picture what failure meant."

Nellie also met "the second Laura Bridgman" at the school that afternoon. "She excels Laura in cleverness," the director whispered of the young Helen Keller. "One day she'll be known as the marvel of her age."

Pulitzer believed that two writers assigned in the same area would do their competitive best. If he brought in other girl stunt reporters, Nellie would be obliged to outdo herself, time and again. They all would. This led to more and more outlandish stunts. Soon stunt girls were so commonplace that the *World* began lumping them under one byline, "Meg Merrilies" (though not Nellie—it was too late to humble her this way; her byline was too popular). The name drew on a fictional gypsy from a popular novel by Sir Walter Scott, and, subsequently, a poem by John Keats:

> *Old Meg she was a Gipsy,*
> *And liv'd upon the Moors:*
> *Her bed it was the brown*
>   *heath turf,*
> *And her house was out of*
>   *doors.*

Among them, these stunt girls steered ships in a storm, rescued a child from a burning building, and jumped in front of a trolley car to lobby for better brakes on public transport. "Sob sisters" sat in on celebrity murder trials, offering up gory details and sympathy where appropriate (to appeal to a female readership). Fevered competition eventually made all the stunts and emotional "splashwork" look ridiculous. The escalating game got old fast, and things became demeaning and embarrassing for the writers, who were, after all, only trying to escape the boredom of writing about ladies' hats.

For Nellie and many other woman writers, if it came down to performing stunts versus covering the fashion and society pages, there was no contest. The challenge was to stay credible.

By 1889, the unprecedented growth of Joseph Pulitzer's *World* was beginning to top off and, alarmingly, circulation even dipped a little. It was unacceptable, and Pulitzer began to gather his great minds together in the evening to hash out story ideas. He needed one that was as splashy as the *World*'s 1885 campaign to fund the Statue of Liberty's pedestal with readers' spare change, a story that would not only get the numbers up again for a day or two but capture the imagination of a fickle public for weeks or months to come. His key editorial staff pitched idea after idea, finally settling on one that would come as no surprise to Nellie.

On November 11, Colonel Cockerill sent her an invitation to embark on the stunt of a lifetime. ❧

PARADING HER PERSONALITY

Respected author Willa Cather took scathing—and satirical, even on the level of spelling—issue with the *World*'s Meg Merrilies in an 1894 article in the *Nebraska State Journal* titled "Utterly Irrelevant":

The *New York World* is undoubtedly a newsy paper, and it undoubtedly possesses two of the best dramatic critics in the country, but it also possesses a young woman who needs the worst kind of boycotting. The young person who calls herself Meg Merrilles is, if possible, more obtrusive and more insane than her predecessor, Nelly Bly. Meg Merrilles claims that she will do "all that may become a man," which would be all well enough if she stuck to it, but she don't; she banks upon her sex to sell stuff that would be simply commonplace if she were a man, but which because she is a woman is absurd enough to be read. She fights a round with Corbett and writes six columns about it, visits a gambling den and takes great credit to herself therefor, allows herself to be run over by a motor car, and explodes in double-column headlines and exclamation points the fact that she took a shock from an electric battery. Now, if Miss Mervilles discovered anything new or threw new light on anything old there might be some excuse for her painful parading of her personality, but she is as totally lacking in originality as she is in self-respect.

Willa Cather, 1875.

9: around the
WORLD

If you want to do it, you
can do it. The question is,
do you want to do it?

Her editor, it turns out, would hand Nellie's own idea back to her. The previous fall, she had proposed to circle the globe faster than the fictional character Phileas Fogg had in Jules Verne's popular 1873 novel, *Around the World in Eighty Days*. She had even gone so far as to visit a travel agent and collect timetables for ships and trains.

It was a good idea, and timely—the *World* wasn't the only New York newspaper itching to send readers on an epic voyage—but the paper's senior staff had balked at the idea of that voyager being Nellie. Business manager George W. Turner complained that a woman would need a chaperone for such a journey. She would require an impractical number of trunks.

Nellie knew she could pull it off, and when she heard rumors that the *World* would send a man instead, she warned the paper's business manager, "Very well . . . start the man, and I'll start the same day for some other newspaper and I'll beat him."

Pausing to look her over, Turner said, "I believe you would."

When she showed up in John Cockerill's office on November 11, he asked, "Can you start around the world day after tomorrow?"

"I can start this minute."

But that night, as if her life hadn't just taken an extraordinary turn, Nellie casually attended a Broadway performance of *Hamlet* with her mother.

In the morning, she visited one of the city's most fashionable dressmakers. She told William Ghormley that she needed a dress by that evening, one that would hold up to constant wear for months. Nonplussed, the expert dressmaker displayed fabric options for a traveling gown, settling on blue plaid broadcloth. They arranged for her to come back at five and try it on. "I always have a comfortable feeling," she later wrote, "that nothing is impossible. When I want things done, which is always at the last moment, and I am met with such an answer: 'It's too late. I hardly think it can be done;' I simply say: 'Nonsense!'"

Nellie skillfully packed a single bag, a carry-on, with wardrobe basics (*very basic* basics), an inkstand, pens, pencils, paper, needles and thread, a flask and drinking cup, and a few other necessities, including the jar of cold cream she refused to sacrifice,

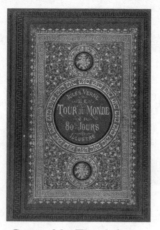

Cover of the French first edition of Jules Verne's Around the World in Eighty Days, *published January 30, 1873.*

which in the end proved "bulky and compromising." She did not pack a revolver, as cautioned.

The *World*, meanwhile, scrambled to pull together her passport and itinerary, fitting her out with English gold, Bank of England notes, and $2,500 in American gold and bills. She would test out this money in various ports to see how widely US currency was accepted. No special travel arrangements were made. The trip would reflect the average travel route around the globe using only the usual lines of commerce.

The newspaper put all its might behind Nellie's voyage but admitted, for drama's sake, when it announced her itinerary, that the whole thing was "pretty on paper." In other words, the odds were slim, and the stakes were high. Any number of obstacles lurked: typhoons, sandstorms, icebergs, mechanical breakdown, not to mention winter storms and other unforeseen, garden-variety delays. Even the most minor holdup could make for a missed connection.

On November 14, 1889, at 9:40

A.M., more than two decades before the first passenger airline would take to the skies, Nellie sailed from Hoboken Pier on the liner *Augusta Victoria*. After all the fanfare and well wishes, when the steamship whistle blew, and she watched her friends and family grow smaller on the pier, she felt momentarily "lost."

Meanwhile, John Brisben Walker, proprietor of *Cosmopolitan* magazine, announced that he would send another young female reporter, a former *World* colleague of Nellie's named Elizabeth Bisland, on a western route in a bid to outpace Nellie on her eastern one. Though Bisland's itinerary was fuzzy, the *World* proposed that the "Misses B" might pass like the proverbial ships in the night, perhaps in Hong Kong. They could enjoy Christmas dinner together! The *World* all but ignored the so-called race, and Nellie, already at sea, had no idea that she was racing against more than time.

The *Augusta Victoria* met with headwinds and stormy seas. "Never

The ocean liner Augusta Victoria around 1890.

having taken a sea voyage before," Nellie expected "a lively tussle with the disease of the wave," and she got one. She spent a portion of her early voyage with her head over the deck rail. Worse still, people were "unfeeling" about seasickness. It was as if they purposely stationed themselves nearby to smirk. "The smiles did not bother me," she wrote, "but one man said sneeringly: 'And she's going around the world!'"

Nellie was a good sport and joined in their laughter, but secretly she thought herself very bold to have set off on such an adventure with no previous experience at sea.

In the end, as ever, she "did not entertain one doubt as to the result."

On calm days, passengers in first and second class passed the time on deck, reading, napping, strolling together in conversation. Meals were lavish when Nellie could keep them down; the average dinner aboard a steamship was typically French and fancy with up to twenty-nine distinct dishes in nine courses. At night, the band played concerts under the stars, and women gathered in the ladies' saloon for dessert and group singing while men, per custom, went off to smoke and drink brandy. Nellie wasn't much for singing, and these hours made her restless. She was itching to reach England and get on with it.

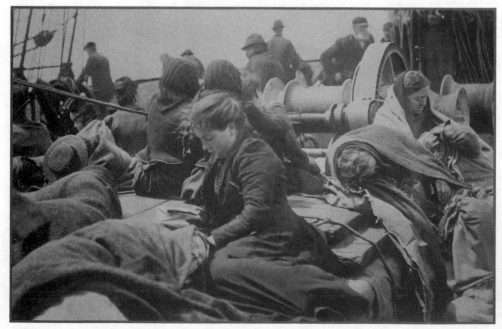

Steerage passengers on the deck of an ocean liner, around 1900.

It's interesting that she doesn't seem to have used some of her down time to explore below decks, where in stark contrast some seven hundred passengers in steerage crowded together in what felt like dark, airless barracks shut off from the rest of the ship by iron doors. Unmarried men, unmarried women, and families bunked in separate quarters but shared bathrooms and sinks. Passengers brought their own bedding, dishware, and utensils aboard. The basins used for washing up and cleaning dishes doubled as the place to empty your stomach if, like Nellie, you suffered the disease of the waves. Needless to say, meals were a single course, often bread and butter for breakfast, or oatmeal and molasses. These passengers were no wealthy vacationers off to explore the continent but people who had fled poverty and oppression in their native lands and were returning home to them with whatever savings they had scraped together in the United States.

Nellie's first proposal, when she went seeking work at the *World*, was that she cross the Atlantic to report on the plight of these passengers firsthand. Now she was crossing that ocean in high style, on a very different errand. She seems not to have noticed those below decks at all or, for that matter, the overworked stokers who shoveled coal into the furnaces of great steamships like the *Augusta Victoria*, now speeding her on her way.

At long last, more than six days later—and sixteen hours past schedule—Nellie stood swaddled in a traveling rug against the damp chill, surrounded by mailbags and fellow passengers excited to be seeing her off, satchel in hand, as the ship docked in Southampton, England. The shrill whistle was lost in a chorus of "Good luck, Nellie!" as the gangplank went down.

The *World*'s London correspondent, Tracy Greaves, met Nellie on the plank with news: Jules Verne himself wanted to see her. She was already behind schedule, but the chance to meet the famous French author who had inspired her voyage was a tempting opportunity, and when Greaves assured her she could fit it into her breakneck schedule if she was "willing to go without sleep and rest for two nights," Bly accepted. ❧

LINES OF TRAVEL

It was still dark as their carriage raced through London in a thick fog. Nellie wouldn't see sunlight until she crossed the English Channel into France. Jules Verne, his wife, and a Paris journalist who would act as translator stood waiting on the platform. "When I saw them," Nellie wrote later, "I felt as any other woman would have done under the circumstances. I wondered if my face was travel-stained, and if my hair was tossed. . . . There was little time for regret." She felt comfortable with the couple at once, though her discourse with Madame Verne was mainly a lot of apologetic smiling since "her knowledge of the English language consisted of 'no' and my French consisted of 'Oui.'"

On the carriage ride to the Vernes' home in Amiens, Nellie glimpsed bright shops, a park, and nursemaids pushing baby carriages, but like much of her journey, her experience of France was fleeting. A shaggy black dog came bounding out when they arrived, and once they were comfortable in the sitting room beside a crackling fire, a "fine white angora cat" settled in Madame Verne's lap. The other journalist went to work translating back and forth. Has M. Verne ever been to America? How did he get the idea for his novel? (Verne had been inspired by a newspaper article.) What would be her line of travel? Nellie had memorized her itinerary, and after she told him—New York to London, Calais, Brindisi, Port Said, Ismailia, Suez, Aden, Colombo, Penang, Singapore, Hong Kong, Yokohama, San Francisco, and then, if all proceeded as planned, a bold homecoming in New York City—he asked why not Bombay, like his hero Phileas Fogg?

Time, she explained. She soon glanced at her watch and realized it was running out. There was only one train to Calais, and "if I missed it I might just as well return to New York the way I came, for the loss of that train meant one week's delay."

Nellie asked to see the great man's study before she went and was surprised, after following him up a spiral staircase, to find that he worked in a very small room with a single window and a flat-topped desk. Apart from a bottle of ink, one penholder, and a manuscript, the desk was bare, and the only other furniture inside was a modest couch. "In this room with these meagre surroundings," she marveled, "Jules Verne has written the books that have brought him everlasting fame." In the library next to the study, Verne revealed a large hanging map with blue marks on it where he had traced Phileas Fogg's journey with a pencil. He now marked out her course, as the others gathered around him, where it differed from Fogg's.

Before Nellie left, as the four clinked glasses of wine, the Vernes wished her "Godspeed," and she felt as if she were leaving behind friends. Her detour had jeopardized her timeline, and she had gone without sleep, but Nellie saw this time as a privilege. "I felt that if I had gone around the world for [the pleasure of meeting them], I shouldn't have considered the price too high."

The French correspondent later wrote of a side conversation he had with Verne. "What do you think?" he had asked the author, "of this idea of a young girl endeavoring to beat your fictitious character's record in a journey around the world?"

"I think it is extremely original," Verne said. "Even for Americans."

Background: Amiens, France, around 1890.
Above right: Jules Verne around 1878.

Strohmeyer & Wyman, Publishers,
New York, N.Y.

Sold only by Underwood & Underwood
New York, London, Toronto Canada, Ottawa Kansas.

The Arab's Shibriyeh.—A Home on the Desert, Egypt.

The Arab's Shibriyeh.—A Home on the Desert, Egypt.
Copyright 1896, by Underwood & Underwood.

10: SIGHTSEEING
(and other inconveniences)

> My head felt dizzy and my heart felt as if it would burst. Only seventy-five days! Yes, but it seemed an age and the world lost its roundness and seemed a long distance with no end, and—well, I never turn back.

Nellie's impatience and determination during her trip sometimes made her edgy. Of the unavoidable two-hour layover that followed her visit with the Vernes, she grumped, "There are pleasanter places in the world to waste time in than Calais." On the train from Calais, France, to Brindisi, Italy, she complained, "I might have seen more while traveling through France if the car windows had been clean." In response to the cold—and to the rumor that the train she was on had been held up the week before by Italian bandits—she quipped, "If the passengers then felt the scarcity of blankets,

they at least had some excitement to make their blood circulate."

She had eagerly looked forward to the Italian countryside, that "balmy sunny land," but her hopes were dashed. "It is a most extraordinary thing," one of the train guards told her. "I never saw such a fog in Italy before." Nellie only had one good glimpse—of a gorgeous beach along the Adriatic Sea—when the fog lifted during a station stop.

Arriving two hours late in Brindisi, Nellie transferred to a liner called the *Victoria*, where a rumor soon circulated that she was "an eccentric American heiress, traveling about

Left: A man leading a camel with a tented litter and two passengers on its back through the desert, Egypt, 1896.

with a hair brush and a bank book." This led to at least one marriage proposal, which she politely declined.

When the *Victoria* anchored at Port Said, in northeast Egypt, male passengers armed themselves with canes and the women with parasols against beggars. Offered her choice of weapon, Nellie declined, "having an idea, probably a wrong one, that a stick beats more ugliness into a person than it ever beats out." Her sympathy didn't hold, though. The "hungry greed" of the boatmen clamoring to bring them ashore made her "feel that probably there was some justification in arming one's self with a club." Nellie encountered many beggars along the next few stops, with "outstretched hands" and "plaintive appeals," both adults and children, and her sympathies would continue to ebb and flow.

Hiring a boat with some acquaintances, Nellie went ashore in Aden (modern Yemen) and was delighted to discover a good-humored people with "the finest white teeth of any mortal." Aden natives apparently polished their teeth to perfection with a soft, fibrous wood from a local tree, scraped free of bark.

Another thing that roused Nellie's curiosity was the custom in Aden of bleaching the hair yellow or red with lime juice exposed to hot sun and water. The local women didn't partake, but the look "was considered very smart among the men."

She was held up in Colombo, Ceylon (now called Sri Lanka), and succumbed to sightseeing. One of the street performers who "haunted" the hotel in ragged jackets and turbans showed her a trick she loved: Taking a seed in his fingers, he covered it with a handful of earth. Layering a handkerchief over that, he chanted a moment and picked the cloth away to reveal a green sprout, declaring it too small. He covered and chanted again, unveiling a still larger plant, and so on, until he had a tree "from three to five feet in height."

One snake charmer had to wrestle his lashing cobra back into its basket until blood gushed from the snake's mouth. It wouldn't dance, he admitted. The cobra was too young and "fresh."

When Nellie finally boarded the steamship *Oriental* after three additional days' delay, her patience was again thin. "When will we sail?" she demanded of bystanders, one an elderly gentleman with kind eyes who explained that waiting for the connecting ship, the *Nepaul*—"a slow old boat," which would deliver passengers and mail onto the *Oriental*—had put them behind.

"May she go to the bottom of the bay when she does get in!" Nellie blurted out savagely. "The old tub! I think it an outrage to be kept waiting five days for a tub like that."

Aware that her ill humor had surprised her smiling companions, she imagined herself slinking back to New York ten days behind schedule, shamed and humbled. The mental image made her laugh out loud. "My better nature surged . . . and I was able to say once again, 'Everything happens for the best.'"

In Penang (in modern Malaysia), she visited a temple and drank tea with monks "from childlike China cups" while both parties, without a language in common, smiled incessantly.

Two days out from Penang, Nellie found herself longing for something new to happen. Perhaps an old-fashioned pirate attack?

In Singapore she rode a rickshaw and enjoyed the spectacle of a passing funeral party. The casket, with "probably forty pall-bearers," floated past in a din of fifes, cymbals, tom-toms, and gongs, together with ponies and men bearing banners, Chinese lanterns, and roast pigs on poles.

While in Singapore, she bought herself a souvenir, after resisting all other purchases in her determination to travel light: "When I saw the monkey, my willpower melted." Nellie bargained hard and demanded to know, did the creature bite. The owner said no, taking the animal by the throat and holding it up for her to admire. But how could he bite, Nellie observed wryly as they settled the deal, "under the circumstances"?

During an ongoing monsoon en route to Hong Kong, she weathered the passionate advances of a "mad man" on deck and woke one night to find, to her horror, the sea sloshing over the ship and flooding her cabin with water. "I thought it very possible that I had spoken my last word to any mortal, that the ship would doubtless sink." She almost took comfort in the idea, which would relieve her of having to explain her failure to circumnavigate the globe on schedule. Nellie was beginning to believe she wouldn't "get around in one hundred days." Luckily, the water didn't rise high enough to reach her sleeping berth.

She made no secret throughout the trip of her passion for staying up late and sleeping in. On the way to Hong Kong her rest was disturbed each morning by the sound of a father and toddler in an adjacent room engaged in noisy rituals. "For heaven's sake," Nellie bellowed on the sixth morning, "tell Papa what the moo-moo cow says and let me go to sleep."

The child's parents ignored her for the rest of the trip.

THE OTHER WOMAN

Despite the monsoon and an additional three days' delay, the *Oriental* made up the time lost in Colombo, reaching Hong Kong two days before Nellie's itinerary demanded. She admired the beautiful bay and terraced view of Hong Kong from the deck of the ship, but when she and companions reached the town by sedan chair, she deemed it dirty.

"My only wish and desire was to get as speedily as possible to the office of the Oriental and Occidental Steamship Company to learn the earliest possible time I could leave for Japan and continue my race against time around the world."

When she arrived and inquired, the officer asked Nellie's name, then bluntly informed her, "You are going to be beaten."

"What? I think not," she shot back. "I have made up my delay."

The clerk insisted, with conviction, that she would "lose it."

"I don't understand. What do you mean?" Nellie was beginning to think he was crazy.

"Aren't you having a race around the world?"

"Yes, quite right. I am running a race with Time," she replied.

"Time? I don't think that's her name."

Nellie demanded to know which "her" the poor fellow had in mind.

"The other woman. She is going to win. She left here three days ago."

It was news to Nellie, as her no doubt stunned expression revealed. The man explained about Elizabeth Bisland, and Nellie countered with, "I promised my editor that I would go around the world in seventy-five days and if I accomplish that, I shall be satisfied. I am not racing with anyone."

Left: Hong Kong street scene, 1895.
Above: Journalist Elizabeth Bisland during her around-the-world race against Nellie Bly.

Though Nellie was often invited to dinner or gatherings in her honor, she mostly refused. She didn't have appropriate dinner dress and, well, she was working. The trip was "business" and she considered it her "duty to refrain from social pleasures."

She praised the "youthful look" of people in Hong Kong and rhapsodized generally, in a wink-wink aside to her female readers. "At every port I touched I found so many bachelors, men of position, means and good appearance, that I naturally began to wonder why women do not flock that way," she wrote, referencing the old cry "Go West, young man."

"A most happy time do these bachelors have in the East. They are handsome, jolly, and good-natured. They have their own fine homes with no one but the servants to look after them. Think of it, and let me whisper, 'Girls, go East!'"

Back on the ship, she briefly indulged in quiet daydreaming on deck, but as usual, her restlessness won out, and she scolded herself: "Away with

Geishas in rickshaws: Nara, Japan, 1906.

dreams. This is a work-a-day world and I am racing Time around it."

She spent Christmas in Canton, China, visiting a leper colony "appalling in its squalor and filth." She left that place feeling blue and empty—and homesick: "It was Christmas Day, and I thought with regret of dinner at home."

Nellie ate hers in the Temple of the Dead.

New Year's Eve came on the sea between Hong Kong and Yokohama, Japan, where Nellie joined her shipmates for champagne and oysters and a round of "Auld Lang Syne."

When Nellie asked after her monkey the stewardess informed her, "We have met," and displayed an arm bandaged from wrist to shoulder. Like any proud, oblivious new parent, Nellie demanded to know what the woman had done to provoke her pet.

"I did nothing but scream," the stewardess countered. "The monkey did the rest."

In Japan, Nellie attended a geisha dance performance and was generally impressed by the culture and scenery. "I found nothing but what delighted the finer senses."

As Yokohama harbor receded behind the ship, the band played Nellie on her celebrated way. The chief engineer of the *Oceanic,* she discovered, had emblazoned the engine room with the slogan:

FOR NELLIE BLY,
WE'LL WIN OR DIE.
JANUARY 20, 1890.

11: father TIME OUTDONE

> I wanted to yell with the crowd, not because I had gone around the world in seventy-two days, but because I was home again.

It seemed a promising departure, but on the third day out from Japan, the ship met with a violent storm, one that went on and on, in Nellie's view, with wild headwinds and pitching waves. "If I fail, I will never return to New York," she moaned. "I would rather go in dead and successful than alive and behind time."

"Never mind, little girl, you're all right," the captain told her cheerfully—a variation on the pep talks she received all along her route. "I've bet every cent I have in the bank," he assured her. "Take my word."

In this way, Nellie later wrote, "I was coaxed out of my unhappiness every day by those great-hearted strong tender men."

Back home, the *World* reported to breathless readers that Nellie was even now crossing "the largest extent of water in the universe. . . . Her grit has been more than masculine."

At one point as the storm raged on, Nellie learned that sailors considered monkeys "Jonahs," responsible for bad weather aboard ship. Would she consent to throw hers overboard, someone joked, in the interests of progress? "A little struggle between superstition and a feeling of justice for the monkey followed." Luckily for Nellie's new pet, the *Oceanic* got her into port more or less on time, and it seemed that she would beat Phileas Fogg's fictional record, after all.

The night before they were scheduled to dock in San Francisco harbor, a purser approached her, deathly pale, with news that the ship's "bill of health" had gone missing. Perhaps it had been left behind in Yokohama?

"What does that mean?" Nellie demanded.

"It means," the nervous man told her, "that no one will be permitted to land until the next ship arrives from Japan." That would be . . . two weeks, he added.

"I would cut my throat for I could not live and endure it," Nellie roared—so close and yet so very far from New York and success.

A more thorough search uncovered the report in the doctor's desk, and yet

THOUSANDS OF MIND'S EYES

Today, Wi-Fi allowing, Nellie would tweet about her trip. She would post selfies with scenic backgrounds on Instagram. But with both time and technology so limited, the most she could do was dash off a cable now and then, and these were slow in reaching New York. It was up to her sponsoring newspaper to stoke the fire of interest in her voyage, and the *World* did a bang-up job of it. They mentioned Nellie in every edition of the newspaper from the day she set out until the day the cannons roared to signal her homecoming. Whenever possible, they charted her movements, making readers feel invested in the trip. Her daring enterprise was a club that all *World* readers belonged to, and when Nellie hit US soil again, public excitement exploded.

"Within the last twenty-four hours the interest in Miss Bly's undertaking has increased more than fourfold," the *World* reported just before she docked in San Francisco. Letters and telegraphs began pouring in Thursday another obstacle was overcome. But when the revenue officers boarded the ship the next morning with newspapers, Nellie read of an "impassable snow blockade," one that had halted train travel in the region for a week. Her "despair knew no bounds."

Still, she pressed on. When the tugboat arrived to fetch her, with "no time for farewells," she was delivered into it with her monkey and her baggage, the quarantine doctor shouting down that she must submit to having her tongue examined before she could land. She stuck it out at him. Exasperated, he called back, "All right," as onlookers laughed and cheered, and Nellie waved good-bye.

night from all over the country and from all classes of people: there were Dakota ranchers boasting about the bets they'd made, young boys "gallantly" offering their services as Nellie's escort "from any point that the editor of the *World* may designate," and little girls who signed their letters with "My dearest love to darling Nellie Bly."

"If Miss Bly can find time to read half of these [childish expressions]," the *World* maintained, "her eyes will be moist for a week."

One *World* innovation was to sponsor a sweepstakes inviting readers to guess how long Bly's trip would take to the day, hour, minute, and second. The prize was an all-expenses-paid trip to Europe, and the paper, which received almost a million guesses, reported, "Thousands of 'mind's eyes' are now following Nellie Bly in her trip around the world." Always ready to cash in on its star reporter, the *World* even published a large board game, Round the World with Nellie Bly, modeled on Parcheesi.

When she stepped back onto American soil on January 21, she learned that the *World* had arranged for a special train to spirit her to Chicago on a southern route to avoid the storm and packed snowdrifts.

Nellie called the transcontinental run, or "flying trip," that followed a "glorious ride worthy of a queen." It was a "maze of happy greetings, happy wishes, congratulating telegrams, fruit, flowers, loud cheers, wild hurrahs, rapid hand-shaking and a beautiful car filled with fragrant flowers attached to a swift engine that was tearing like mad through flower-dotted valleys and over snow-tipped mountains."

At long last, she could rest. There was nothing to do now but sit back quietly and wait, read, pet McGinty the monkey, count telegraph poles, or take in the beautiful scenery passing by the train window "swiftly as a cloud along the sky."

"I could hurry nothing," Nellie wrote. "I could change nothing."

Cheering crowds greeted her at every stop, and Nellie "rejoiced with them that it was an American girl who had done it." People praised her sunburned nose and reached out for her hands. One man offered a rabbit's foot for luck, another invited her to Kansas—"we'll elect you governor"—and another, when she answered that she hadn't ridden an elephant in her travels, "dropped his head and went away." People took her success personally, and that, she said, was the best part. "They were all so kind and as anxious that I should finish the trip in time as if their own personal reputations were at stake."

Telegrams found their way to her, some addressed—as simply as Santa's at "the North Pole"—to "Nellie Bly, Nellie Bly's train." In Chicago, a cable that had missed her in San Francisco caught up with her: "M. and Mme. Jules Verne address their sincere felicitations to Miss Nellie Bly at the moment when that intrepid young lady sets foot on the soil of America." (The great writer was probably doubly pleased with Nellie in that she brought fresh publicity to his novel: *Around the World in Eighty Days* was reissued in more than ten new editions in France before Nellie even completed her journey.)

A group of "good-looking" Chicago Press Club reporters whisked her off the train during a station stop to visit their club.

A stationmaster in Columbus, Ohio, said he couldn't remember ever having seen such pandemonium, not even the year President Cleveland visited or President Harrison before that. Women made up at least half the crowd mobbing the station.

By this point in the journey, McGinty—suffering a bout of flu and uncharacteristically docile in his cage—had become "a present from the rajah at Singapore."

People wondered had she encountered Elizabeth Bisland during her travels? She had not, Nellie said dismissively, claiming never to have considered her challenger—even now delayed by storms on the Atlantic—a rival. "We are both on an errand," she added, taking the professional high ground.

As the train raced from Chicago to Philadelphia, Nellie got to work dictating to a stenographer. The *World* would publish her remarks on Sunday to coincide with several pages of newsprint dedicated to her arrival.

In Pennsylvania, at a station stop near the end of the journey, Mary Jane was escorted through the teeming crowd and several train cars to a special reserved car called the *Beatrice*.

The *World* treated readers to a tender glimpse of her reunion with her globe-trotting daughter, describing how Nellie's sunburned face lit up when she saw Mary Jane. The crowd of men parted to let her pass, and Nellie rushed forward into her mother's waiting arms.

"Oh, Nellie!" Mary Jane cried, holding on tight, and Nellie answered, "Mother! I'm so glad!"

"That meeting was a sacred thing," wrote the *World*. The door closed, and "the rest of it was their secret."

Nellie jumped down onto the platform at Jersey City at 3:51 on January 25, 1890. Three timekeepers stopped

An engraving of Nellie Bly's Jersey City homecoming.

their watches. Cannons fired at Battery Park and Brooklyn's Fort Greene Park. Nellie waved her cap.

The journey had taken 72 days, 6 hours, 11 minutes, and 14 seconds, and she had—the *World* crowed—broken every record. "For the first time in the history of the world there will be recorded the circumnavigation of the earth by a woman without guide, escort, or attendant."

From Jersey City, Nellie took a ferry to Manhattan and was delivered with great fanfare to Park Row, where the celebrations continued.

With the front-page headline "Father Time Outdone," the newspaper devoted a whopping four pages of the January 26 issue to Nellie's exploits, including mention of the ill-fated Elizabeth Bisland, who was still on her way to New York aboard the *Bothnia*, "one of the slowest ships of the Cunard line," one "wallowing in the trough of the yeasty Atlantic." Though she wasn't able to hold her own against Nellie, the paper added Miss Bisland would be remembered. The *World's* staff wished her well.

In the spirit of good sportsmanship, *Cosmopolitan* editor John Brisben Walker, who had sponsored Bisland, delivered Nellie a basket of rare roses at Park Row.

Sweepstakes entrant F. W. Stevens of New York beat out 927,432 other contestants by predicting Nellie's time almost to the instant. (The *World* had pledged to record it to a fifth of a second; Stevens anticipated an extra two-fifths of a second.)

At just twenty-five years old, Nellie was an international celebrity, possibly the most famous woman on the globe she had just circled. Music halls rang to the tune of Nellie Bly songs. Nellie Bly housecoats, caps, cakes, and canned goods hit the market. Her sensible traveling outfit—blue skirt-and-jacket combo, boldly checked wool coat, and jaunty cap—was so popular that women imitated it for years.

More than a celebrity reporter now, Nellie was an American icon. Her feat captured public imagination at a time when steamships and transcontinental railroads were crisscrossing the planet, making it feel small and accessible.

Call it pluck, spunk, feistiness, or just daring, but a young American female had embarked alone on a 21,700-mile journey without a chaperone or a spare dress, and other woman reporters watched with interest.

In a signed editorial in the *Philadelphia Inquirer*, reporter Dorothy Maddox wrote: "The *World*, in sending its bright little correspondent upon such a novel, yet hazardous mission, has with one unique stroke accomplished more for my sex than could have been achieved in any other way in a decade . . . open[ing] the door that leads to success in every branch of the world of letters."

When a *San Francisco Chronicle* interviewer called her feat remarkable, Nellie replied, "Oh, I don't know. It's not so very much for a woman to do

O Nellie Bly, upon a 'Bi;
Around the planets in the sky,
Pursues the stars,outstrips their gleams,
And races comets (in her dreams.)

who has the pluck, energy and independence which characterize many women in this day of push and get."

Some observers, including an old suitor, James Metcalfe, who published a parody of her trip in *Life* magazine, and her friend and mentor Erasmus Wilson in an affectionate article in *Pittsburgh Commercial Gazette*, questioned the importance of Nellie's feat and fame.

In "What Doth It Profit a Girl to Girdle the Earth?" Wilson focused on the stunt as a business triumph (not just for Nellie and her newspaper but also for other media outlets that made a profit on the story, as well as the travel and fashion industries). He understood the restlessness that drove his friend through her now-celebrated life.

"Why doesn't every newspaper girl do something great or unusual," he asked, "thereby making for herself a name and fortune that will last? Because they are not all built that way . . . Nelly Bly never could work problems according to the book. She couldn't do it in school nor could she do routine newspaper work."

Nellie Bly advertising card published by Wilson Biscuit Company of Philadelphia, "manufacturers of Faultless Biscuits, Cakes, and Crackers."

AIN'T I A YOUNG TEACHER

As an adult, Nellie told readers that "threatening heart disease" had forced her to leave boarding school in her youth. To brave even one more year, her doctors warned, would be to risk her life. No matter how determined she was to continue her studies, the future celebrity "didn't want to die."

She may have been embarrassed to admit what really happened: her family ran out of tuition money. She simply couldn't afford to remain in school.

In truth, Nellie never was much of a scholar anyway. A lofty-sounding family history called *Chronicles of the Cochrans: Being a Series of Historical Events and Narrative in Which the Members of This Family Have Played a Prominent Part* credits Pink with gaining "more conspicuous notice for riotous conduct than profound scholarship." She was, simply put, "rather wild."

Her classmates thought of Pink as scrawny and plain if quick with a comeback. One friend, Lillie Elliott Myers, told her grandchildren how she had envied Pink her long white stockings, while her friend always claimed to wish the stockings were black like everyone else's. Did Lillie believe her? Should we? Did Pink Cochran want to be like other girls and just fit in? Or did she already feel the restless pull of an uncommon life that would lead her around the world? In a way, the decision was made for her.

At fifteen, when Pink decided to support her divorced mother and sidestep disgrace by pursuing a career in teaching, boarding school seemed the one escape for a clever girl of reduced standing.

The state normal school at Indiana was just fifteen miles east of Pink's

Apollo home. Over the four years since it was established, the school had become the pride of the county, with its spacious campus and celebrated faculty. But could Pink afford to go? Apollo's distinguished banker, colonel Samuel Jackson, looked after Pink's inheritance from her father. Pink paid him a call and argued her case. She needed a goal, she said, and a fresh start. She argued well: six months after signing her mother's court testimony as "Pinkey E. J. Cochran," Pink enrolled in boarding school under the name "Elizabeth J. Cochrane," losing her longtime nickname and tacking an elegant silent 'e' onto her surname.

Two weeks into her stay, Pink dashed off a penciled note to her brother Charles. She asked after their mother and described her room, her roommate, and her studies, which included grammar, reading, writing, arithmetic, drawing, and spelling. "I teach in model school," she wrote, forsaking grammar for a laugh. "Ain't I a young teacher. Be a good boy and remember me in your prayers."

Indiana Normal boasted art facilities, gas lighting, steam heat, hot and cold running water, a reference library, a gym, a huge chapel, and a bookshop. There was carpeting on the floors of the women's dorms. For less than a full term, Pink had access to everything she could have wanted or needed to feed her eager mind and aspirations, and then—just as quickly—she didn't.

With the term almost over, Pink wrote to Jackson to arrange for the trip home. He sent ten dollars, warning her to spend it wisely. Funds were dwindling. At home, Pink studied her accounts and suffered a shock. She was out of money. With Mary Jane in no position to help financially, and with no other source of support, Pink withdrew, bitterly disappointed. When she came of legal age, she would sue her prominent guardian for mismanaging the portion of her father's money set aside for her, but for now she was just a girl without a plan.

Her schooling had ended almost before it began. Teaching would be out of the question now. Pink needed another way to make her mark on the world.

Background: Art class sketching, State Normal School, Indiana, Pennsylvania, around 1910.

Nellie was an original, in other words, and would be remembered that way, even if her trip would not "benefit science," in Wilson's words, or "add to our knowledge of the world. It was mainly an advertisement for the *World* and for the daring little adventuress."

Nellie's account of the trip, published in four installments in the *World* and later reprinted as *Nellie Bly's Book: Around the World in Seventy-Two Days*, was wildly successful. When people asked how she planned to rest and recuperate, she claimed she didn't need to. She was sorry the trip was over. She would go home, introduce her pet, McGinty, to his new apartment, and get back to work.

She couldn't have anticipated what happened next.

The monkey, released from his cage, broke every dish in her apartment. And despite the phenomenal success of her romp around the world, Nellie's publisher offered no raise. No bonus.

Her fame, the *World* maintained, was her reward.

Furious and insulted, Nellie quit. 🐦

Right: Excerpt from Nellie Bly's 1891 letter to her friend Erasmus Wilson.

SUSPENDED HOSTILITIES

I'll have much to show you—The pretty things presented to me on my trip around the world, lots of books and photographs, the cleverest parrot, the most wonderful monkey, and the wisest Skye terrier in the world. So come before the monkey knocks the life out of the parrot and the dog shakes the impishness out of the monkey, for not one is congenial and friendly with the other and they are in a constant state of suspended hostilities.

12: industries of
MAGNITUDE

> Nellie Bly is the busiest person in New York, man or woman. In fact, there are few persons of the billion and a half that toil and groan on this round earth that are so occupied as she.

—The *World*, March 8, 1896,
in a story proposing
that Nellie Bly would
fight for Cuba

Nellie's familiar byline was missing from New York papers for three years. During that time, she took a stab at writing dime-novel fiction in installments. But making up stories from scratch wasn't her strength.

Her brother Charles had died young in 1890—at just twenty-eight years old—and Nellie helped care for his wife and two children. Rumors that had circulated after her trip—that she would marry a young doctor named Frank Ingram or that she planned to donate McGinty to the menagerie in Central Park—proved to be just rumors.

She embarked on her new career with customary enthusiasm, but seven months into serial writing she confessed in an overdue reply to Erasmus Wilson: "I meant to answer . . . at once but I suddenly became a victim of the most frightful depression that ever beset [a] mortal." Nellie hadn't done "a stitch of work for weeks," she admitted, urging her friend to visit; she was "growing fat."

Pulitzer's *World*, meanwhile, was undergoing intense change with editors (including Colonel Cockerill) going and coming, and when a new editor took over the profitable Sunday edition in September of 1893, he invited Nellie back. Feeling financial

Left: Nellie Bly, around 1900. Background pattern is a patent for an "improved milk can" filed on behalf of Bly under her business name, E. C. (Elizabeth Cochrane) Seaman, 1902.

pressure and the failure of her fiction experiment, Nellie accepted.

Her first "comeback" story, an interview with "Emma Goldman and Other Anarchists," made the *World*'s front page, and ran under a triumphant headline: "Nellie Bly Again."

For her interview with Goldman, Nellie visited the young radical in prison. Detained in the Manhattan Tombs on charges of inciting a riot, Goldman did not, Nellie argued, fit the public stereotype. "You have read of her as a property-destroying, capitalist-killing, riot-promoting agitator. You see her in your mind a great raw-boned creature with short hair and bloomers, a red flag in one hand,

a burning torch in the other." In fact, Nellie proposed, Goldman was "a modern Joan of Arc" who spoke and wrote six languages. She was also passionate and sincere, "a little bit of a girl . . . with a saucy, turned-up nose."

Both women had grown up poor and had fought their way up from the bottom, but while Nellie got famous and successful writing about the lives and struggles of women and the working poor, Goldman had ended up in a reeking jail cell. Nellie was one of the first and the few to show Goldman sympathy and respect. When she asked about marriage and whether her young subject believed in it as the peak and solace of a woman's life, Goldman replied: "I was married . . . when I was

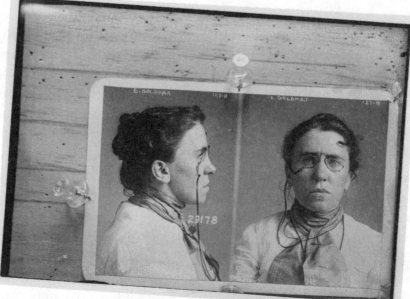

Anarchist Emma Goldman several years after Bly interviewed her.

scarcely seventeen. I suffered—let me say no more about that. I believe in the marriage of affection. That is the only true marriage. If two people care for each other they have a right to live together so long as that love exists."

In October Nellie persuaded her editor to send her to Saratoga for the New York State Democratic Convention. How would the Tiger—a nickname for the political leaders of Tammany Hall, the headquarters of the Democratic party—receive her? Walt McDougall's accompanying cartoon shows Nellie standing tall, smartly dressed, and leading a cowering tiger by a chain. As Brooke Kroeger puts it in her biography of Nellie: "The story is pure Bly, confident, unintimidated, acting her role as celebrity reporter in the company of powerful men: in short, her idea of a good time."

But like other woman reporters of the time (though more and more were bristling about it), Nellie was still assigned her share of stunt or filler material alongside the challenging or politically charged stories she preferred. Her reputation would only serve her so far. She spent ten days investigating "The Midnight Band of Mercy," for example, "An Odd Gathering of Curious Women Who Are Devoting Their Lives to Alleviating the Suffering of Itinerant Cats." She spent a long night in an allegedly haunted house in Woodport, New Jersey, with her dog Paddy and two pistols.

After her comeback at the *World*, Nellie successfully supported her mother, her sister Kate, and Kate's daughter, Beatrice, with the family shuttling between a farm in White Plains and a snug apartment at 120 West Thirty-Fifth Street in Manhattan. Her relationship with her older brother, Albert, was often strained, but Nellie was devoted to family and offered shelter and support to all of her siblings and their offspring at various points in time.

Only four months in, though, she wondered if returning to the newspaper game had been a mistake. Amusing though some of her stunts were—and unlike Meg Merrilies, she usually managed to shape them to her own ends, righting wrongs, exposing culprits, and satisfying her curiosity along the way—Nellie could only measure her accomplishments against the yardstick of the past. Was she fulfilling her promise, her purpose? She wasn't too shy to pose such questions out loud, and her grumblings eventually led the trade magazine *The Journalist* to remind readers why Nellie had left the paper in the first place: "The *World* understands how to manipulate women."

WHAT TOOK SO LONG?

Pink was between nine and fourteen years old during her mother's terrible remarriage, but at this formative time, the women's rights movement was also picking up steam around her native Pennsylvania.

Educational opportunities for women were improving, a far-reaching marriage-property law protected women's interests, and even political advancement must have seemed tantalizingly within reach; in 1876 in Philadelphia, at a patriotic ceremony to honor the centennial, Susan B. Anthony had seized the platform in Independence Square to recite a suffragette's declaration of independence.

But all this advancement was lost on young Pink's alcoholic stepfather, Jack Ford.

On New Year's Eve, 1878, Mary Jane brought her children to a church party held at Odd Fellows' Hall on Apollo's Main Street. Ford may have forbidden the outing, or perhaps his wife failed to ask his opinion in the first place. But it's easy to imagine Mary Jane's horror and embarrassment—and the wary shock on the faces of Pink and her siblings—when Ford burst into the festive room waving a loaded pistol and ranting that he would kill his wife if she were "the last woman on earth." The crowd of merrymakers must have parted in surprise with men moving to herd their families away from the drunken intruder or rushing forward to subdue him.

The incident no doubt made for juicy small-town gossip the next day. Mary Jane stayed with friends while her husband simmered down, but this was far from unusual behavior for him. The family had endured it before and would again. The couple reunited, but nine months later Ford lashed out at the dinner table. He smashed furniture and rammed walls, cracking the plaster. His boot left a gaping hole in the rocking chair. The next night, cursing and howling, Ford flung Mary Jane's fresh-laundered clothes into the wet backyard. At dinner he sliced the meat and hurled a bone at his wife, who hurled it back, at which point he produced a loaded pistol from his pocket while Pink and Albert formed a human wall and Mary Jane bolted for the exit. While the family sheltered with neighbors, Ford nailed shut every accessible door and window, using a ladder to get in and out.

A week later Mary Jane managed to access the empty house. It had been ransacked. She rented another and moved her children to safer ground. Ford, who must have known the game was up, skipped town.

On October 14, Mary Jane sued her husband for divorce.

Today, in a case like this, we might ask, "What took so long?" But in 1875, this was a bold, even scandalous move. There had been only eighty-four divorces in Armstrong County over the previous ten years, very few filed for by the wife. Divorce was seen as shameful, demeaning, and, above all, impractical. It wasn't done, except in drastic circumstances.

Eleven family friends and neighbors stood up that day, bearing first-hand witness to Ford's "cruel and barbarous treatment," his drunkenness, "ungovernable temper," and "pugilistic demonstrations." There were other accusations, too, from failing to provide for his family and extorting money to keeping a loaded gun under the bed and regularly threatening to murder his wife. Mary Jane lived in dread. One neighbor reported that when Mrs. Ford arrived one night seeking safety, she hid "behind the chimney for fear he would shoot her through the window."

Albert and Pink, ages nineteen and fourteen, offered testimony of their own. Their stepfather daily called their mother vile names the prim Mary Jane would not herself repeat in polite company. "Ford has been generally drunk since they were married," Pink explained. "When drunk, he is very cross and cross when sober . . . The first time I seen [sic] Ford take hold of mother in an angry manner, he attempted to choke her."

The young woman who had seen her mother driven to tears and exile time and again signed the court transcript "Pinkey E. J. Cochran."

NELLIE BLY AND THE GHOST

—✳—

Armed with Two Pistols, She Passes the Night in That Haunted House at Woodport, N.J.

—✳—

THE SPOOK NOT AT HOME.

—✳—

Waiting for the Appearance of the Minton Spectre and That Diaphanous Hand.

—✳—

ONE MILE FROM ANY HABITATION.

—✳—

Strange Antics of a Frolicsome Door Laid Bare During the Vigil While the Wind Was Howling.

—✳—

A HUNT IN THE GLOOMY ATTIC.

—✳—

A Rather Courageous Venture by Miss Bly That Many Men Would Shrink from Undertaking.

Headlines from an 1894 article by Nellie Bly in the New York World.

Nellie soon filed a series of reports that would be among the strongest of her career. In Chicago, railroad workers had been on strike for eight weeks against the Pullman Palace Car Company, resulting in riots and looting, with buildings and trains going up in flames. With the nation deep in recession and many joining the ranks of out-of-work people, the protest swelled. The situation was urgent, with the rail system on the verge of collapse. Federal troops were on hand to control the chaos when Nellie arrived during the last week of the strike. She entered Chicago bitterly set against "rioters and blood-thirsty strikers," but her view soon flipped. She arrived in the "model" town of Pullman determined to tell the story of the strike from the opposing perspective, but after talking with downtrodden families of the strikers, her three-part series carried headlines like, "What the Women Say," "Nellie Bly Talks with the Wives and Mothers Whose Children Are Starving to Death,"

"Low Wages and High Rents," and so on. It was a compelling angle on the emergency, one no other New York newspaper had taken.

Success in Chicago might have improved her professional outlook, but a letter to old pal Erasmus Wilson hinted instead at sadness, resignation, and disappointment. "I used to have such hopes," she wrote. She was working only "off and on," she confessed, with "a worse temper than ever."

Her articles continued to appear in the *World* on Sundays, but with the low caliber of filler assignments and the mood of antic competition, Nellie couldn't seem to shatter the perception—whether inside *World* offices or out in the world at large—

that woman journalists were less than credible.

Nellie took refuge in her farm in White Plains, where she now spent most of her time. In a letter evoking shady lawns, orchards, and a menagerie with a horse, a cow, five dogs, and sixty-four chickens (no mention of a parrot this time . . . or a monkey), she asked Wilson, "Can you picture me as a farmer?"

Her relationship with *Sunday World* editor Morrill Goddard was rocky at this point, and when an editor at the *Chicago Times-Herald*—impressed with Nellie's recent Midwest coverage—offered her a job in February 1895, she took it.

But after just five weeks in Chicago, Nellie abruptly quit the *Times-Herald* to marry a seventy year-old millionaire from Catskill, New York. She had met Robert Livingston Seaman, a sworn bachelor, at a dinner at a Chicago hotel just two weeks before, and their union set everyone reeling. Colleagues wondered if it was another stunt! *Town Topics* joked

The Illinois National Guard monitors strikers during the Pullman Railroad Strike, 1894.

that Nellie was staging another of her "fakements" and tried out imaginary headlines like "Is Marriage a Failure? Nelly Bly Tries It with a Good Old Man!!"

Seaman's heirs took a less whimsical view. They insinuated that Nellie was a gold digger with "devious motivation." The match soon had tongues wagging in his community, but Nellie held hers, at least on this topic. Her marriage was private. She returned to New York to prepare for a life as Mrs. Seaman, one divided between her husband's three magnificent properties: a brownstone in

Nellie Bly, age thirty, raised eyebrows when she married seventy-year-old millionaire Robert Livingston Seaman after a two-week courtship.

Manhattan's exclusive Murray Hill district, a summer home on the Hudson River, and a three-hundred-acre farm in the rolling Catskills.

Did Nellie get what she expected—and felt she deserved—from the marriage? Things didn't begin well. Seaman failed to honor his promise to support Nellie's mother and sister. He stirred up unrest between his brother and his wife over finances. He was a suspicious man, "unaccountably jealous," and all that first summer Nellie believed he was having her followed. By way of counterattack, she refused to have dinner with him.

They had been married less than seven months when Nellie confirmed her suspicions by tricking the snoop her husband hired and having the man arrested. Seaman told reporters that he had indeed paid an employee—not a private detective—to discreetly observe his wife's evening activities. "I have a right to know where my wife takes her dinner," Seaman pronounced. "She refuses to dine at my table and I wished to know where she did dine. Now that's all there is to it."

In 1895 he wrote up a will that left his wife very little security while his nieces (and a mystery woman) would claim more. This must have hit Nellie hard and brought back memories of Apollo and the indignities suffered by her widowed mother.

To assert independence again—both financial and marital—Nellie decided to do what she did best: she got back to work.

In 1896, after an epic bout of hirings, firings, and desertions at Joseph Pulitzer's *World*, a new editor took over the *World* Sunday supplement. An old friend and champion of Nellie's, Arthur Brisbane, invited her back. The timing, a few months into her rocky marriage, couldn't have been better, and Nellie eagerly accepted. Her first headline in three years carried a familiar headline: "Nellie Bly Again."

Nellie was now a seasoned veteran. One of her first "comeback" assignments was to cover the National American Woman Suffrage Convention in Washington, DC, and she turned in a surprisingly personal interview with Susan B. Anthony, one of the movement's iconic leaders. As usual, the interview revealed almost as much about Nellie as it did about her subject. For instance, certain delegates were distinctly lacking in fashion sense, in her opinion, and she couldn't help but say so. "Dress is a great weapon in the hands of a woman if rightly applied. It is a weapon men lack, so women should make the most of it."

Nellie investigated police corruption during this period, challenging Commissioner Theodore Roosevelt's plan to close homeless shelters for women in police stations. As in the past, insightful interviews and hard-hitting investigative journalism alternated with stunt and filler assignments like "Nellie Bly as an Elephant Trainer" with its front-page sketch of Nellie high on the back of a huge elephant. Nellie loved animals, luckily, so perhaps stories like this

Susan B. Anthony around 1890.

NELLIE BLY AS AN ELEPHANT TRAINER.

Novel and Thrilling Experience With the Immense Animals in Their Winter Home.

PERILOUS RIDE ON THE IVORY TUSKS OF FRITZ.

I tried to train an elephant last week. The elephant was scarcer. So was I. Neither of us mentioned it at the time. But I have thought of it since and doubtless so has he.

I have always had an intense fondness for elephants. This fondness has necessarily placed at a distance. I once hoped to own an elephant and—

It can readily be understood why I wished to see the proprietors of the "Greatest Show on Earth," when they had brought eight new elephants to America.

But they refused to sell even the little elephant. They said, however, I might go to Bridgeport and make acquaintance of their elephants and training them. With joy and gladness in my heart I accepted their offer.

I was with great eagerness I followed a guide through the door into the elephants' training quarters.

It was a little low room, with a ring at one end, and at the other, chained in a semi-circle, were eight of the cunning baby elephants I ever saw.

The room was hemmed by a large, round stove. Near it stood a barrel filled with water and a little beyond, on a pile of straw, lay three immense black and white Danes, which sprang the length of their chains and barked furiously as I...

[text continues, illegible]

"Here's been making it easy for her," said Mr. New[man]...

held genuine interest for her. She was a pro and made each story her own with enthusiasm and honest insight—in recounting her elephant ride, she confessed, "I merely did it because I hadn't courage to say I was afraid"—that kept her fans loyal and interested to hear what she had to say next.

In one of her last efforts from this period, Nellie vowed to join forces with Cuban rebels against bloody Spanish rule, "arranging to add a new terror to war!" the *World* trumpeted. "You could say that it would be impossible for a slender, comparatively frail young woman to do such a fearsome thing. But that is because you are not thoroughly acquainted with Nellie Bly."

Nellie's pledge to "raise up such friends for poor, harassed Cuba as no nation fighting for liberty has ever had before" never took form. Instead, she up and quit her job at the

World again and sailed to Europe with the husband she had previously refused to have dinner with. It may be that Nellie's Cuban mission rattled Seaman and softened his stance toward his assertive young partner. On November 17, 1896, he drew up a new will, naming Nellie sole executor and increasing her share of holdings. She now had the control and financial security that she had so long craved for herself and her family.

The couple had been overseas for three years and were arranging to return to New York to seek new management for Seaman's troubled business when Nellie got dire news. Her thirty-two-year-old sister, Kate, had contracted tuberculosis and died suddenly in July.

Heartbroken and fierce with grief, Nellie sailed to New York ahead of her husband. The family spent summers in the Catskills, and a local weekly newspaper painted a startling picture of her emotional state when she arrived home: Nellie apparently built a funeral bonfire in the yard with her sister's belongings, setting fire to "beautiful silk dresses," jewelry, mattresses, tapestries, and a wagon—items the reporter, who deemed it a "silly performance," felt could have been sold to profit the needy.

Nellie ordered the paper to retract its intrusive comments or she would sue. (It did.)

To distract from the overwhelming loss of her sister, Nellie decided to become more involved with her husband's business, the Iron Clad Manufacturing Company. A number of family members lived with her at the time in Seaman's four-story brownstone in Manhattan, including Mary Jane, brothers Albert and Harry and their wives, Kate's daughter, Beatrice (now in Nellie's charge), and, off and on, her brother Charles's two teenage children. Nellie had always gone to great lengths to see to the health and well-being of her family, financial and otherwise—from insisting that Seaman provide for them in her marriage agreement to underwriting the educations of her nieces and nephews. She was as bent on their success as she was on her own. Perhaps, on some level, she blamed her mother for her relatively passive approach to managing a family, one that had left Nellie and her siblings vulnerable as children and at times, especially where her older brother Albert was concerned, at odds as adults.

But Nellie's involvement with Iron Clad, which made milk cans, boiler tanks, garbage cans, enamelware, and other such useful stuff, made it possible for her to take over after her husband died of heart complications following a 1904 accident (Seaman was struck by a carriage while crossing the street).

Nellie had devoted much of her career as a journalist to listening to working-class people and asserting their rights, and now, as president and owner of Iron Clad, she modernized her company in line with her beliefs. She fitted out its headquarters in Brooklyn with showers, a dining room and library, a gym and bowling alley, and a small hospital. Recreation was offered on Saturdays, including lectures. The company even had a baseball team. Nellie paid her workers guaranteed weekly salaries instead of offering piecework.

She had a business card made up, featuring her picture and the tagline: "The Iron Clad factories are the largest of their kind and are owned exclusively by Nellie Bly, the only woman in the world personally managing industries of such a magnitude."

It seemed that her new career as a giant of industry would lead Nellie down entirely new and unexpected paths, but yet again fate brought her byline back to New York newspapers. ❧

WEARING THE SIDEWALK THIN

The man who would become Joseph Pulitzer's most rigorous competitor and help launch a turn-of-the-century circulation war, William Randolph Hearst, was a generation younger and everything Pulitzer wasn't: American-born, a child of careless wealth, Hearst had been kicked out of Harvard for bad behavior, gravitating toward the newspaper business instead. He watched Pulitzer's innovations at the *New York World* with interest. His future rival—who used sensational headlines, grisly crime stories, pictures (including color comics, inspiring the term "yellow journalism"), and games and contests—had seized on an all-new way to make it rich through journalism, Hearst believed. Hearst would glide into New York and buy the *New York Journal* in 1895, then steal Pulitzer's entire Sunday *World* staff, starting with his most celebrated daredevil reporter, Morrill Goddard, who had found fame as a London correspondent assigned to the Jack the Ripper story. Hearst paid a whopping $35,000 for Goddard alone.

Furious, Pulitzer bought them back, only to find his restored staff cleaning out their desks again and trekking back to the *Journal*. Hearst had outmaneuvered him twice. Staff started joking that the sidewalk between the two news headquarters would soon wear thin.

This highly competitive environment formed the backdrop of Nellie's 1896 comeback.

Above: William Randolph Hearst, 1906.

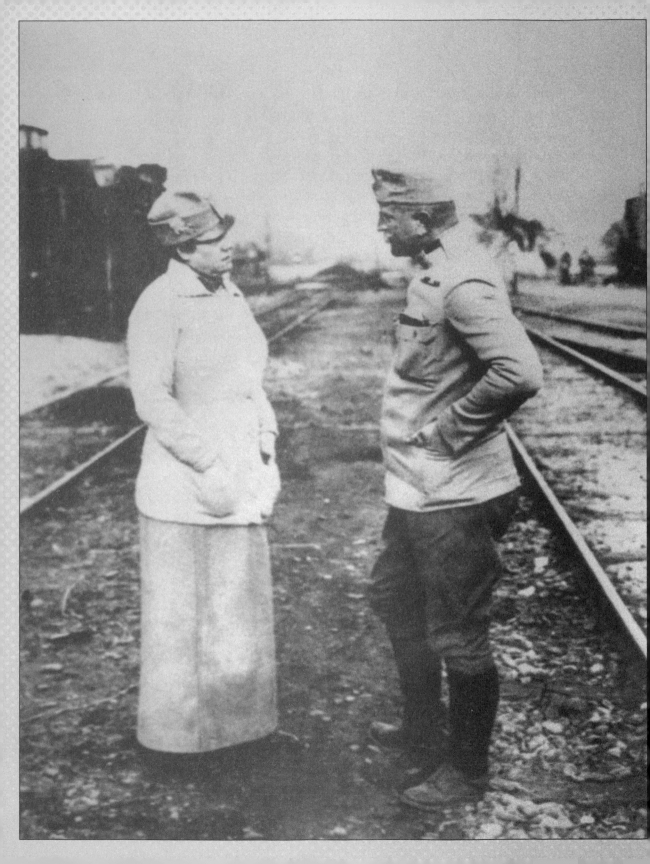

13: GOOD fights well FOUGHT

> I almost despaired of getting out
> of the trench. At that spot it
> was fully eight feet high and as
> slippery as a greased pole. I had
> no nails in my shoes, and as I
> made a step I slid back.

"**I** cannot blame myself enough for not having learned banking methods and commercial accounting when I first went into the Iron Clad," Nellie confessed later, after it became clear that her company's finances were in disarray. "However I never in my life had taken any interest in money for itself, and financial details bored me."

It turned out that some employees had been scamming her and had skimmed up to two million dollars from the company's accounts, dragging Nellie into bankruptcy and other court cases that went on for years.

On August 1, 1914, she set sail for Austria, partly because she needed to rest and lie low, and partly to seek help from a wealthy friend in Vienna.

Her three-week trip turned into a five-year stint as a war correspondent.

Four days before her ship set sail to Europe, Austria declared war on Serbia. Germany invaded Luxembourg.

World War I, or the Great War, was under way, and Nellie arrived in Austria ready to bear witness.

In October she was one of just a handful of foreigners admitted into the battle zone, and the only woman. Two months later, she had made her way to the front lines. She visited the Russian and Serbian front,

Left: Reporting from the front lines for the New York Evening Journal, *Nellie Bly speaks with an unidentified Austrian officer, 1914.*

encountering difficult terrain, grim weather, forbidding mountains, and roads and passes blocked with mud and snow. Exposure killed thousands of troops that winter, and Nellie saw the suffering firsthand.

She was briefly detained on suspicion of being a British spy and had to dive into a trench during a Russian shelling attack. She climbed muddy, bare hills without a single tree or shrub left standing or a single blade of grass.

Everywhere was mud—smooth, shiny, and "more slippery than ice." She told of men under fire for weeks in rain and cold, of terraces that looked like "a series of half-dug graves" in readiness for the next round of battle, of pits filled with the dead, of men digging bullets out of their flesh with pocketknives. "Come, look, reader, with me!" she urged, turning her attention to an emaciated soldier in a Red Cross hospital. Begging for his children ("the hollow, black eyes turned again to search mine. I could not endure their question. I had no

A horrific scene of WWI trench warfare like those Nellie Bly witnessed on the front lines.

answer to give") just moments earlier, the man now died before her eyes.

"This is only one case," she lamented. "Travel the roads from the scene of battle; search the trains; wounded, frozen, starved thousands are dying by agonizing torture—not hundreds, but thousands. And as they die thousands are being rushed into their pest-filled trenches to be slaughtered in the same way."

Nellie's urgent impressions appeared in the *New York Evening Journal* (where Nellie's old editor and friend Arthur Brisbane now worked), and every headline carried her name: "Nellie Bly on the Firing Line," "Nellie Bly at Front," "Nellie Bly at the Scene of Slaughter," though their publication was staggered and delayed for weeks at times, or even months.

When she returned to New York in February 1919, both her personal and business lives were in a sorry state. Nellie had left her money, property, and remaining business prospects in Mary Jane's care, but her mother had relinquished them to her brother Albert, leaving Nellie all but penniless. Nellie and Albert had been at odds for years, and he refused to be reasoned with.

"I struggled all my life to gain comfort and independence for my mother," Nellie wrote in a heartbreaking appeal to Erasmus Wilson in March 1919, "and that mother deserts me and crushes me."

She sued her older brother for control of the business but had to make a living meanwhile.

In May, her byline once again appeared in the pages of the *New York Evening Journal*. Nellie covered prizefights in this period and the grisly confession of a young murderer. She contributed a column to the editorial page, dispensing advice on marriage, motherhood, and other popular subjects, and airing her opinions on issues like gambling, birth control, and capital punishment.

She also began to put her column to practical use to help right social wrongs, assisting out-of-work mothers and abandoned children in need of loving families. "Little Orphan Girl," her youthful pen name, seems both fateful and ironic—Nellie became so associated with finding homes for needy children that in December 1919 an infant boy turned up at Grand Central Station with a note pinned to his clothing: "To Somebody—For the love of Mike, take this kid. He is too much for the family. Give him to Nellie Bly of the New York *Journal*."

During 1920 and 1921 Nellie was plagued with bronchitis. She had trouble breathing, and coughed continually, but kept up her usual brisk pace, ignoring the advice of her doctors and the medicines they prescribed.

On January 9, 1922, she was admitted to St. Mark's Hospital in New York with pneumonia.

She died at 8:35 A.M. on January 27, 1922, at the age of fifty-seven, and New York papers sang her praises. Her friend and champion Arthur Brisbane devoted his *New York Evening Journal* editorial to her memory. Nellie was "THE BEST REPORTER IN AMERICA," he wrote, "and that is saying a good deal."

She had led a useful life, he said, and took with her "the memory of good fights well fought and of many good deeds never to be forgotten by those that had no friend but Nellie Bly."

The same day that she entered the hospital, the *Evening Journal* ran what would be her last published work, a column reflecting on her own extraordinary life. "Are we not governed by destiny over which we have no control?" she asked readers, comparing the lives of two women, "or did each make her own life?"

A rhetorical question, but while Nellie saw her share of struggle and challenges she also, as her *New York Times* obituary put it, "went down into the sea in a diving bell and up in the air in a balloon." She went around the world, and "every one who read newspapers followed her progress."

Nellie owned her life from the beginning, it seems, and if we circle back and stand beside her in front of that mirror in her humble West Ninety-Sixth Street lodgings—a very young woman alone and penniless in a city of millions, jittery with dread and excitement, rehearsing her lunacy at the beginning of a great adventure—it could be argued that this was the defining (deciding?) moment in a long life of daring.

What will be yours? 🐾

AUTHOR'S NOTE

In his 1922 obituary, Arthur Brisbane called his friend Nellie Bly "THE BEST REPORTER IN AMERICA." But what makes a good reporter?

While many Americans still get their news through TV and other traditional channels, the explosion of mobile devices and social networks allows us to witness, even stage, a revolution in real time or watch hurricane winds rip off the door of a trailer on the other side of the globe. Multimedia and lightning-fast connection make immediacy and transparency the norm, and breaking news can reach us through a citizen journalist with a cell phone as easily as a professional reporter trained to interpret it.

Trained journalists vow to pursue truth and follow a few basic ground rules in the process—nine, according to the Pew Research Center's Journalism Project, including an obligation to verify all claims. But even among experienced journalists, there are as many ways to arrive at news as there are people reporting it.

What sort of reporter was Nellie? As biographer Brooke Kroeger notes, Nellie Bly was an expert interviewer, willing and equipped to charm her way into her subjects' lives and secrets. At various points in her career, she was also a columnist, social reformer, travel writer, and war correspondent. She even tried her hand at fiction.

But today we know her best for her stunt work, which falls under the umbrella of investigative journalism. Investigative journalists root out scandal, corruption, and breach of trust; expose questionable government and corporate practices; and track key social, political, or economic trends with a goal of mobilizing the public. They're our watchdogs and our canaries, and they're critical to a healthy democracy.

What puts stunt reporting in a subcategory of its own is that it takes place undercover, on the sly. In Bly's era, newspapers didn't think twice about employing deception to get the story, but today these methods are often dismissed as subjective or unethical.

Does undercover reporting distort or entrap? Do two wrongs make a right?

"Going undercover is meant to be the journalism of last resort," Brooke Kroeger points out in *Undercover Reporting: The Truth About Deception*. Culprits thrive in the dark. We wear our best face in public, and misbehaving governments, companies, and institutions are no exception. As Bly learned when she went back to Blackwell's with investigators after her exposé, conditions can be cleaned up or concealed under scrutiny. It's what happens when nobody's looking that makes for news, and sometimes stealth is still the best way—the one way—to bear truthful witness.

While Bly was a pioneer, she wasn't the first investigative or stunt journalist. Even before the Civil War, reporters on the staff of Horace Greeley's *Tribune* went undercover in the South to report on the abuses and inhumanity of slavery, risking a tar-and-feathering or worse if exposed. She wasn't the first or only woman doing such work, either. Ida Tarbell's groundbreaking *History of the Standard Oil Company* challenged John D. Rockefeller, one of the most powerful men in the world, by exposing questionable corporate practices. The term "muckraker" was coined later to describe writers like Tarbell, Upton Sinclair, and Jacob Riis, who were committed to social change.

Bly's asylum exposé shocked the nation and led to major reforms, but it also made her a household name. By the time she returned from her trip around the world, she was as famous, if we think in terms of scale, as any pop diva or movie star trending on Twitter today. She not only got the scoop, she *was* the scoop, and her celebrity may be what makes her feel, a century later, curiously modern. It's not a stretch to imagine her posting strategic selfies on Instagram, or tweeting from the airport. Would she have made use of new media? All evidence points to her feeling right at home in our culture of celebrity. Elizabeth Jane Cochrane was a reporter first, but she was also a personality, a persona—the plucky, itinerant Nellie Bly—and her reporting style echoes in more recent work by writers like "gonzo" reporter

Hunter S. Thompson, who rode with the Hell's Angels and was nearly pummeled to death for his trouble.

Bly was a feminist, but a playfully irreverent one (picture her as a child strutting around in pink, a rare bird among drab brown ducks . . . or lecturing Susan B. Anthony about fashion sense). She liked to be admired and to flirt (a ridiculous number of the men she encounters in her exploits are proclaimed "handsome" or "good-looking"). She once told her friend and mentor Erasmus Wilson that her goals were to "crash a New York newspaper, fall in love, marry a millionaire, and reform the world," and it seems she mostly succeeded.

She was also a committed social reformer who sometimes lacked sensitivity. Her travelogue displayed her humor, will, and energy but also flashes of the casual racism common in her day, and disregard for cultures unlike her own.

Bly could be as petulant as she was tender, as frivolous as she was socially earnest, as funny and self-deprecating as she was proud and haughty. A wonderfully stubborn determination echoes all through her articles, her choice of subjects, and her single-minded pursuit of adventure and excellence. Savvy till the end, despite tragedy and setbacks, she always trusted herself and stood by her talent and her rights with hard-won confidence.

Nellie Bly was a hero, but she was also a person. All heroes are just this in the end, and it's what makes them extraordinary—in spite of everything, their fundamental and flawed humanity, they achieved great things. Two moments in her story stand out for me and speak to her courage and empathy: that New Year's Eve when her stepfather burst into a church function waving a pistol at her helpless mother, and the moment when Bly paused on the asylum lawn, having come out to say good-bye to her "suffering sisters," and thought, "for ten days I had been one of them. . . . It seemed intensely selfish to leave."

It would have been easy to give in to despair at such times or to surrender to a life she did not choose for herself, but instead Nellie Bly used her gifts to turn the tide—for herself and countless others.

Deborah Noyes

SOURCE NOTES

1: The Gods of Gotham

"Dear Q.O. . . . Look out for me. Bly": *Eighty Days: Nellie Bly and Elizabeth Bisland's History-Making Race Around the World* by Matthew Goodman, p. 16.

"neat and catchy": *Nellie Bly: Daredevil, Reporter, Feminist* by Brooke Kroeger, p. 43.

"obtain the opinion of the newspaper gods of Gotham": Goodman, p. 21.

"'Are you opposed to women as journalists, Mr. Dana?'. . . . Women are no good, anyway.": Ibid., pp. 22–24.

2: More Than Anyone Would Believe

"Write up things as you find them, good or bad . . . truth all the time": *Around the World in Seventy-Two Days and Other Writings* by Nellie Bly, edited by Jean Marie Lutes, p. 19.

"Energy rightly applied and directed . . . anything": Kroeger, p. 85.

"Never before in civilization . . . tender beauty": *The Spirit of Youth and the City Streets* by Jane Addams, p. 5.

"our growing conviction . . . nor do we regard it safe for any lady to answer such unseemly utterances": *The Devil in the White City* by Erik Larson, p. 11.

"had to do a great deal of talking": Goodman, p. 24.

"journal dedicated to the cause of the people . . . evils and abuses": *Pulitzer: A Life* by Brian Denis, p. 65.

"ACCURACY . . . THE FACTS!": *The Murder of the Century: The Gilded Age Crime That Scandalized a City and Sparked the Tabloid Wars* by Paul Collins, p. 16.

"chronic smile": Lutes, p. 19.

"You can try . . . more than anyone would believe": Kroeger, p. 86.

"smile no more . . . only get in": Goodman, p. 28.

3: Strange Ambition

"Who could tell but that the strain . . . never get back": Lutes, p. 22.

"When evening came . . . slowly and sadly": Ibid., p. 21.

"the longest day I had ever lived!": Ibid., p. 24.

"the repulsive form charity . . . lonely evening": *Ten Days in a Mad-House* by Nellie Bly, p. 6.

"fit . . . sympathy and kindness there are in the world": Lutes, pp. 24–29.

"unchangeable fate . . . past was present": *Ten Days*, Bly, p. 9.

"pass over the river to the goal . . . mentally wrecked sisters": Lutes, p. 28.

"greatest night . . . face to face with 'self.'": *Ten Days*, Bly, p. 9.

"'Yes' . . . 'makes my head worse,'": Lutes, p. 35.

"a free American girl": Goodman, p. 15.

"Mexicans have never been represented correctly . . . never-failing kindness": *Six Months in Mexico* by Nellie Bly, p. 70.

4: You Won't Get Out in a Hurry

"And so, I passed by second medical expert . . . I ever had before": Lutes, p. 43.

"in a sagacious manner": Ibid., p. 36.

"'Tell me' . . . care of her": Ibid., p. 43.

"'Have you just found out' . . . wrecked": Ibid., pp. 48–49.

"fearful creatures . . . skillful than charming": Ibid., p. 50.

"We saw, with pleasure . . . to any but excellent persons": Margaret Fuller in *Writing New York: A Literary Anthology* collected by Phillip Lopate, p. 117.

"disgracefully overcrowded . . . lunatic": Kroeger, p. 87.

"other cancer spots of modern Manhattan": Ibid., p. 86.

"abandoned . . . thieves and prostitutes": *American Journal of Psychiatry*, "The Lunatic Asylum on Blackwell's Island and the New York Press" by Samantha Boardman and George J. Makari, p. 581.

"a tomb of living horrors": *Ten Days*, Bly, p. 25.

"'What is this place?' . . . 'where you'll never get out of'": Lutes, p. 50.

5: Into the Madhouse

"I had some faith in my own ability as an actress . . . And I did": Lutes, p. 19.

"by four expert doctors . . . bolts and bars of a madhouse": Ibid., p. 52.

"as rational as any I ever heard": Ibid., p. 53.

"How can they say I am insane merely because I allowed my temper . . . when they get angry": *Ten Days*, Bly, p. 42.

"what your last pug dog . . . and be amply repaid": Lutes, pp. 6–8.

"dissolute habits . . . wretched": Kroeger, p. 43.

"because she had a fondness for other men than himself": *Ten Days*, Bly, p. 41.

"suffering sisters . . . carelessness be excused": Lutes, pp. 53–54.

"I made no attempt . . . crazier I was thought to be": *Ten Days*, Bly, p. 4.

"He gave the nurse more attention . . . 'up in this manner'": Lutes, p. 55.

"chattering foolish nonsense to invisible persons . . . please the patients": Ibid., pp. 57–58.

"the evenings pass very pleasantly . . . horrors!": *Ten Days*, Bly, p. 45.

"slightly spoiled . . . in my slice so didn't eat": Lutes, pp. 64–67.

"horrible messes . . . prayed for death": Ibid., pp. 67–68.

"one of the craziest women in the ward . . . Shut up, or you'll get it worse": Ibid., p. 59.

"high in the centre . . . you won't get it": Ibid., p. 60.

"tired of labor and longing for something new . . . who shall defend?": Kroeger, p. 45.

"I had always been told factory girls . . . as in a parlor": Nellie Bly, "Our Workshop Girls: Pretty
    Females in the Wireworks," *Pittsburgh Dispatch*, February 22, 1885, in Macy, *Bylines*, p. 21.

"smelt like laudanum . . . whole night for one drop": *Ten Days*, Bly, p. 42.

"weaving tales and creating heroes and heroines": Kroeger, p. 14.

"roast to death . . . 'What can I do?'": Lutes, p. 61.

6: She Who Enters Here

"What, excepting torture, would produce insanity quicker than this treatment?": Lutes, p. 66.

"dangerous eruptions . . . pulled and jerked": Lutes, p. 63.

"comical . . . such as bathers wear at Coney Island": *Ten Days*, Bly, p. 35.

"She is one of the incurables . . . Buchanan's eldest son": "A Visit to the Lunatic Asylum on
    Blackwell's Island," *Harper's Weekly*, p. 186.

"The aspect of nature . . . fancies which oppress them": "Blackwell's Island Lunatic
    Asylum," *Harper's New Monthly Magazine*, p. 273.

"[in] the upper halls a good view . . . glimmering in the city": *Ten Days*, Bly, p. 44.

"spotted coming out of the water at what is now Long Island City": "Doing Time on the
    River" by Christopher Gray, *New York Times*, February 9, 2012.

"the light of hope and reason have gone out together": *How the Other Half Lives* by Jacob
    Riis, p. 259.

"old, gray-haired women talking aimlessly to space . . . No fate could be worse": *Ten Days*, Bly, p. 36.

"A file of women . . . with the river in sight": Riis, p. 259.

"'While I was there,' . . . done about it": *Ten Days*, Bly, p. 44.

"WHILE I LIVE . . . LEAVETH HOPE BEHIND": Ibid.

"Here is a class of women sent to be cured? . . . mental and physical wreck": Lutes, pp. 66–67.

"laughed savagely": *Ten Days*, Bly, p. 38.

"Mrs. Cotter here showed me proofs . . . handful": Lutes, p. 81.

"make ugly remarks . . . my other nine were exactly the same": Ibid., p. 80.

"pounced on her and slapped her . . . fingers on her throat": Ibid., p. 72.

"except to scold . . . gossiping": Ibid., p. 76.

"exciting the violent patients . . . pleas for release?": Ibid., p. 79.

"I have described my first day . . . same": Ibid., p. 67.

"offer and give assistance": Kroeger, p. 55.

"impatient to work along at the usual . . . newspapers": Ibid., p. 59.

"They plough, harrow, reap . . . wicked strife of this wicked world!": Goodman, p. 11.

"in compliments": Ibid., p. 12.

"one long-drawn-out five o'clock . . . else": Ibid., p. 9.

"new unfortunates to be added . . . marks of attention": Lutes, p. 72.

"it awakened a big interest . . . 'questions.'": *Ten Days*, Bly, p. 45.

7: After an Item

"BEHIND ASYLUM BARS . . . Feminine 'Amateur Casual'": Lutes, pp. 18–19.

"The insane asylum on Blackwell's Island . . . impossible to get out": Ibid., p. 82.

"'Don't give me away' . . . 'Keep still'": Ibid., p. 71.

"get violent . . . and hair": Ibid., p. 82.

"I talked with her daily . . . Stop it": Ibid., p. 78.

"You have no right . . . delusions": Ibid., p. 79.

"The way the mob rushed me . . . hold-up": Kroeger, p. 93.

"I had looked forward . . . leave them to their suffering": Lutes, p. 83.

"with pleasure and regret . . . sane as I was and am now myself": *Ten Days*, Bly, p. 4.

"found the jurors to be gentlemen . . . august presences": Ibid.

"We went on a clean new boat . . . for the benefit of the insane": Ibid.

"sent to asylums on certificates . . . out of the way": Kroeger, p. 95.

"Your naughty kid . . . pretty big girl": Ibid., p. 101.

8: Stunts and More Stunts

"I have read with some amusement . . . story-teller of the age": Kroeger, pp. 109–110.

"plucky": Ibid., p. 95.

"Nothing was too strenuous . . . dangerous venture": *Bylines: A Photobiography of Nellie Bly* by Sue Macy, p. 36.

"I don't think it had the desired effect . . . deprived": "Deaf, Dumb, and Blind," by Nellie Bly, *The New York World*, February 17, 1889.

"Never having failed . . . what failure meant": "From Jersey Back to Jersey," by Nellie Bly, *The New York World*, January 26, 1890.

"the second Laura Bridgman . . . marvel of her age": "Deaf, Dumb, and Blind," Bly.

9: Around the World

"If you want to do it . . . do you want to do it?": Lutes, p. 147.

"'Very well' . . . 'I believe you would'": Goodman, p. 74.

"'Can you start' . . . 'I can start this minute'": Ibid., p. 76.

"I always have a comfortable feeling . . . 'Nonsense!'": Lutes, p. 147.

"bulky and compromising": Kroeger, p. 141.

"pretty on paper": Goodman, p. 77.

"lost": Lutes, p. 152.

"Never having taken a sea voyage . . . one doubt as to the result": Ibid., pp. 154–155.

"willing to go without sleep and rest for two nights": Ibid., p. 161.

"When I saw them . . . 'Oui'": Ibid., pp. 168–169.

"if I missed it I might just as well return . . . week's delay": Ibid., p. 172.

"In this room with these meagre surroundings . . . everlasting fame": Ibid., p. 176.

"'Godspeed' . . . 'even for Americans'": Ibid., pp. 177–178.

10: Sightseeing (and Other Inconveniences)

"My head felt dizzy and my heart . . . I never turn back": Lutes, p. 152.

"There are pleasanter places . . . Calais": Ibid., p. 179.

"I might have seen more . . . been clean": Ibid., p. 181.

"If the passengers then felt the scarcity . . . blood circulate": Ibid., p. 182.

"It is a most extraordinary thing . . . Italy before": Ibid.

"an eccentric American heiress . . . plaintive appeals": Ibid., pp. 191–194.

"the finest white teeth of any mortal . . . among the men": Ibid., pp. 201–202.

"from three to five feet in height . . . fresh": Ibid., p. 217.

"'When will we sail?' . . . 'happens for the best'": Ibid., pp. 220–221.

"from childlike China cups": Ibid., p. 225.

"probably forty pall-bearers . . . under the circumstances?": Ibid., pp. 229–230.

"mad man": Ibid., p. 232.

"I thought it very possible . . . hundred days": Ibid., p. 234.

"For heaven's sake . . . let me go to sleep": Kroeger, p. 157.

"My only wish and desire . . . 'mean?'": Lutes, p. 238.

"'Aren't you having' . . . social pleasure": Ibid., pp. 240–241.

"youthful look . . . 'Girls, go East!'": Ibid., p. 243.

"Away with dreams . . . Time around it": Ibid., p. 249.

"appalling in its squalor and filth": Ibid., p. 256.

"It was Christmas Day . . . home": Ibid., p. 257.

"'We have met' . . . 'the monkey did the rest'": Ibid., p. 259.

"I found nothing but what delighted . . . 1890": Ibid., p. 267.

11: Father Time Outdone

"I wanted to yell . . . home again": Lutes, p. 281.

"'If I fail' . . . 'take my word'": Ibid., p. 268.

"I was coaxed . . . justice for the monkey followed": Ibid., p. 269.

"'What does that mean?' . . . 'All right'": Ibid., p. 271.

"glorious ride worthy of a queen . . . mountains": Ibid., pp. 272–273.

"M. and Mme. Jules Verne . . . soil of America": Ibid., p. 279.

"good-looking": Ibid., p. 278.

"a present from the rajah . . . 'both on an errand'": Kroeger, p. 170.

"Within the last twenty-four hours . . . moist for a week": Lutes, p. 270.

"Thousands of mind's eyes . . . world": Ibid., p. 190.

"swiftly as a cloud . . . nothing": Ibid., p. 274.

"rejoiced with them . . . done it": Ibid., p. 273.

"dropped his head . . . 'Nellie Bly's train'": Ibid., p. 276.

"sunburned face . . . their secret": Ibid., p. 172.

"For the first time in the history . . . attendant": Ibid., pp. 280–281.

"one of the slowest ships of the Cunard line . . . yeasty Atlantic": Macy, p 43.

"The *World*, in sending its bright little correspondent . . . world of letters": Goodman, p. 97.

"Oh, I don't know . . . push and get": Kroeger, p. 167.

"Why doesn't every newspaper girl do something great . . . daring little adventuress": The Quiet Observer, *Pittsburgh Commercial Gazette*, January 27, 1890.

"threatening heart disease . . . didn't want to die": Goodman, p. 5.

"more conspicuous notice for riotous conduct . . . scholarship": Ibid., p. 4.

"rather wild": Kroeger, p. 13.

"I teach in model school . . . remember me in your prayers": Ibid., p. 24.

12: Industries of Magnitude

"Nellie Bly is the busiest person . . . as she": *The New York World*, March 8, 1896
(Kroeger, p. 289).

"I meant to answer . . . growing fat": 1891 NB letter to Erasmus Wilson.
http://tps.waynesburg.edu/documents/430-nhd-2013-nellie-bly-primary-source-set/
file (#14).

"I'll have much to show you . . . suspended hostilities": Ibid.

"You have read of her as a property-destroying . . . So long as that love exists": "Nellie Bly
Again: She Interviews Emma Goldman and Other Anarchists," *The New York World*,
September 17, 1893. http://dlib.nyu.edu/undercover/nellie-bly-again-she-interviews-
emma-goldman-and-other-anarchists-new-york-world.

"the last woman on earth": Kroeger, p. 18.

"cruel and barbarous treatment . . . the window": Ibid., p. 19.

"When drunk, he is very cross . . . choke her": Ibid., p. 20.

"The story is pure Bly . . . her idea of a good time": Ibid., p. 216.

"NELLIE BLY AND THE GHOST . . . Undertaking": *The New York World*, February 4,
1894. http://www.nellieblyonline.com/herwriting.

"The *World* understands how to manipulate women": Kroeger, p. 226.

"rioters and bloodthirsty strikers": Ibid., p. 235.

"Can you picture me as a farmer?": Ibid., p. 241.

"fakements . . . 'Good Old Man!!'": Ibid., p. 262.

"devious motivation": Ibid., p. 261.

"unaccountably jealous": Ibid., p. 268.

"I have a right to know where my wife . . . to it": Ibid., p. 272.

"Dress is a great weapon . . . make the most of it": Goodman, p. 36.

"The Iron Clad factories are the largest . . . magnitude": Kroeger, p. 309.

"I cannot blame myself enough for not having learned banking . . . bored me": Ibid., p. 329.

"I struggled all my life to gain comfort . . . crushes me": Macy, p. 54 (from a letter to
Erasmus Wilson, March 29, 1919, Carnegie Library of Pittsburgh).

13: Good Fights Well Fought

"I almost despaired . . . I slid back": Lutes, p. 287.

"more slippery than ice . . . Half-dug graves": Ibid., p. 288.

"Come, look, reader, with me! . . . slaughtered in the same way": Ibid., pp. 298–299.

"To Somebody—For the love of Mike . . . the New York *Journal*": Ibid., p. 303.

"THE BEST REPORTER . . . no friend but Nellie Bly": Kroeger, pp. 509–510.

"Are we not governed by destiny . . . her own life?": Ibid., p. 505.

BIBLIOGRAPHY

Addams, Jane. *The Spirit of Youth and the City Streets*. New York: Macmillan, 1909.

Bly, Nellie. "Among the Mad." *Godey's Lady's Book* 18, no. 703 (January 1, 1889).

———. *Around the World in Seventy-Two Days and Other Writings*. Edited by Jean Marie Lutes. New York: Penguin Classics, 2014.

Boardman, Samantha, MD, and George J. Makari, MD. "The Lunatic Asylum on Blackwell's Island and the New York Press." *American Journal of Psychiatry* 164, no. 4 (April 2007): 581.

Brian, Denis. *Pulitzer: A Life*. New York: John Wiley & Sons, 2001.

Collins, Paul. *The Murder of the Century: The Gilded Age Crime That Scandalized a City and Sparked the Tabloid Wars*. New York: Crown, 2011.

Davenport, W. H. "Blackwell's Island Lunatic Asylum," *Harper's New Monthly Magazine* 32 (December 1, 1865): 273. http://harpers.org/archive/1866/02/blackwells-island-lunatic-asylum/.

Goodman, Matthew. *Eighty Days: Nellie Bly and Elizabeth Bisland's History-Making Race Around the World*. New York: Ballantine Books, 2013.

Gray, Christopher. "Doing Time on the River," *New York Times*, February 9, 2012 p. RE7. http://www.nytimes.com/2012/02/12/realestate/streetscapes-the-penitentiary-on-roosevelt-island.html?_r=0.

Kroeger, Brooke. *Nellie Bly: Daredevil, Reporter, Feminist*. New York: Times Books, 1994.

———. *Undercover Reporting: The Truth About Deception*. Evanston, Ill.: Medill School of Journalism/Northwestern University Press, 2012.

Larson, Erik. *The Devil in the White City: Murder, Magic, and Madness at the Fair That Changed America*. New York: Crown Publishers, 2003.

Lopate, Phillip, ed. *Writing New York: A Literary Anthology*. New York: Washington Square Press, 1998.

Macy, Sue. *Bylines: A Photobiography of Nellie Bly*. Washington, D.C.: National Geographic Society, 2009.

Riis, Jacob. *How the Other Half Lives*. New York: Scribner, 1914.

"A Visit to the Lunatic Asylum on Blackwell's Island." *Harper's Weekly* (March 19, 1859): 186.

Further Reading

Berdy, Judith, and the Roosevelt Island Historical Society. *Roosevelt Island*. Images of America. Charleston, S.C.: Arcadia, 2003.

Geller, Jeffrey L., and Maxine Harris. *Women of the Asylum: Voices from Behind the Walls, 1840–1945*. New York: Anchor Books, 1994.

Lutes, Jean Marie. *Front-Page Girls: Women Journalists in American Culture and Fiction, 1880–1930*. Ithaca, N.Y.: Cornell University Press, 2006.

Webliography

American Experience, "Around the World in 72 Days." A companion website to the 1997 PBS Home Video (released on DVD in 2006, WGBH Boston). http://www.pbs.org/wgbh/amex/world/.

Bly, Nellie. *Six Months in Mexico*. New York: American Publishers Corporation, 1888. http://digital.library.upenn.edu/women/bly/mexico/mexico.html.

———. *Ten Days in a Mad-House*. New York: Ian L. Munroe, Publisher, 1887. http://digital.library.upenn.edu/women/bly/madhouse/madhouse.html.

Cather, Willa. "Utterly Irrelevant," *Nebraska State Journal*, October 28, 1894, p. 13. The Willa Cather Archive. http://cather.unl.edu/j00087.html.

Edison, Thomas. "Panorama of Blackwell's Island, NY." An eerie glimpse of Blackwell's Island circa 1903. Available at Library of Congress. http://www.loc.gov/item/00694366.

Groppo, Martha. "Uncovering Nellie Bly." *Kaleidoscope* 10 (2011). http://uknowledge.uky.edu/kaleidoscope/vol10/iss1/41.

Nellie Bly: Online Resources at the Library of Congress, compiled by Kathryn Funk, The Catholic University of America. http://www.loc.gov/rr/program/bib/bly/.

Nellie Bly: The Pioneer Woman Journalist. Arthur Fritz's comprehensive Nellie Bly site includes PDFs of many of her original articles, as well as other useful resources. http://www.nellieblyonline.com/index.php.

Undercover Reporting. A fascinating collaborative project that grew out of research for *Undercover Reporting: The Truth About Deception* (2012) and collects "many decades of high-impact, sometimes controversial, mostly US-generated journalism that used undercover techniques." An indispensable database for anyone interested in Bly or other journalists who practiced "deception for journalism's sake." Brooke Kroeger and NYU Libraries. http://dlib.nyu.edu/undercover/.

ACKNOWLEDGMENTS

This book owes its origins to my colleague and friend Matt Phelan. Matt introduced me to Nellie Bly in his graphic novel *Around the World*, pointing me down a path to a preoccupation that would eventually become this book. Much has been written about Bly's biggest "stunt" (and I can't recommend Matt's concise visual narrative enough). No account of her life can ignore that epic journey. But what resonated most for me were Bly's hungry beginnings and the asylum story. So with Matt's blessing and encouragement, I put my emphasis there.

Thanks also to my oldest friend, Lisa Goodfellow Bowe, a tireless, insightful reader; to my agent and friend, Jill Grinberg, who as ever got what I hoped to accomplish from the beginning; to Jen Hunt, who originally and enthusiastically acquired the project for Penguin; to publisher and editor Ken Wright, who graciously took the book under his wing at Viking; to editor extraordinaire Alex Ulyett; and to Kate Renner, Janet Pascal, Tricia Callahan, and the rest of the staff at Viking.

Last but not least, thanks to Matthew Goodman, whose lively *Eighty Days: Nellie Bly and Elizabeth Bisland's History-Making Race Around the World* was a narrative revelation, and to journalist and biographer Brooke Kroeger, whose rich and meaty *Nellie Bly: Daredevil, Reporter, Feminist* is the authoritative source for all things Nellie Bly. My book wouldn't exist without hers.

PICTURE CREDITS

INDEX

Note: Page numbers in *italics* indicate images.

A master of escape and illusion, Harry Houdini was a man of many talents. But one challenge eluded him . . .

Turn the page to get a sneak peek at Deborah Noyes's next biography, *The Magician and the Spirits*, and prepare to wonder: do the dead return?

ONE

Harry and Bess Houdini, Spirit Mediums

"To me it was a lark."~*Harry Houdini*

In the late nineteenth and early twentieth centuries, vaudeville—which brought touring novelty acts together on one stage—was the most popular form of entertainment in American cities.

But in remote small towns, where the vaudeville tours wouldn't go, traveling medicine shows and their hodgepodge of players parked their wagons and staged a humbler sort of performance.

The formula was simple: performers took over a street corner, produced musical instruments, and made a racket. Once a crowd gathered, the show's pitchman or "doctor" stepped up on a platform and sold his miraculous potions or elixirs. Often he invited the audience back to a local auditorium or music hall for more marvels and "medicine" the same evening.

In late 1897, in need of steady work, twenty-three-year-old Harry Houdini and his young bride, Bess—both struggling variety performers—signed on for a fifteen-week tour with "Dr." Thomas Hill's California

Concert Company, a typical traveling Midwest medicine show, at twenty-five dollars a week.

The company, which included Swiss bell ringers, a German comedian, and the many-talented Keatons (family of future silent-film star Buster Keaton), gathered on dusty street corners in Kansas and Oklahoma territory to draw crowds. Houdini (billed as the "Great Wizard") thumped a tambourine, Bess (the "little vocalist") sang, and when enough curious onlookers had gathered, Dr. Hill announced the evening's show and went to work peddling bottled potions.

The season started out well, but at some point audiences began to dwindle. Dr. Hill had heard of other Midwestern shows drawing crowds with séance and mind-reading routines. Would Houdini want to develop a psychic act of his own?

The Great Wizard had seen a few spirit demonstrations in New York and had no high opinion of them. But for a magician with a mind for mechanics, they would be easy to duplicate, and if Houdini could help the show prosper, it was worth a try.

Before a performance one evening in Garnett, Kansas, he visited the

Bess and Harry Houdini in their first year of marriage, 1894.

local cemetery, "accompanied by the sexton and the oldest inhabitant of the town." He surveyed the graves, jotting down names and ages from the stones. "I had a notebook," Houdini later recalled in a lecture exposing such deceptions, and if the words carved in marble or

A medicine-show pitchman attracts a crowd in Huntingdon, Tennessee, 1935.

granite said too little, "the sexton would tell me the missing data, and the old Uncle Rufus would give me the scandals of everyone sleeping in God's acre."

Houdini spent the day mingling with townsfolk and asked discreet questions. People were only too happy, he learned, to gossip about themselves and their neighbors.

The afternoon crowd had already seen Houdini escape leg irons

☞ The Houdinis

After a brisk courtship of three weeks, Harry Houdini married Wilhelmina Beatrice "Bess" Rahner, a slight pixie of a girl who sang in an act called the Floral Sisters.

Though Harry's mother accepted the bride at once, Bess's mother, a Catholic, couldn't forgive her daughter for marrying into a Jewish family, and shunned Bess for nearly a decade.

The honeymoon on Coney Island was "cheap" but "glorious," said

Bess. Billed as the Houdinis, the newlyweds now became partners onstage as well as off.

Harry and Bess were devoted for life, despite a few bumps in the road, and he showered her with gifts and little love notes, addressed to "Darling One and Only" and "Precious Lump of Sweetness."

"Every morning," Bess recalled, "I would find a dear funny little Message like [this] on my pillow."

and handcuffs, and Dr. Hill had hinted, too, at the young man's extraordinary gift for communicating with the dead. Intrigued, much of the same crowd—and quite a few newcomers—flocked to the local opera house that night to see and hear Houdini in action. He gave them what they came for. Hurling off the ropes that bound him in his chair, he strode downstage as applause faded and the audience grew hushed and uneasy.

In a low, thrilling voice, Houdini mused about the spirit world. Like other performers of the day who included psychic themes (telepathy, hypnosis, mediumship) in their acts, he primed the audience. He closed and opened his eyes. He trembled and gasped as if sensing an invisible presence. Words were coming through, he said—names and dates. As his gaze roamed the room, his voice caught to build drama. One by one, he delivered "messages" from Beyond, revealing facts and family secrets that only a handful of people in the community could have known.

Houdini and Bess also did a joint mind-reading act. Bess walked into the crowd and took a dollar bill from an audience member, challenging Houdini to divine its serial number. Her husband concentrated with otherworldly intensity and then, as the crowd hummed with excitement, rattled it off, digit by slow digit. It was all a clever trick—the

☞ The Effect

Magicians often buy or inherit the secrets and apparatus, or equipment, of retiring performers who've fallen on hard times, and Houdini got his Metamorphosis trick this way for twenty-five dollars (a heap of cash at the time). The illusion included a "substitution" trunk—a steamer trunk big enough to hold a person, with air holes—a giant curtained cabinet, and instructions.

Houdini would call an audience committee onstage. While they examined the props, he stepped into a black flannel sack inside the open steamer trunk. His volunteers tied and taped the mouth of the bag shut, sealing the knots with wax. They closed and padlocked the trunk, swaddled it in thick, knotted rope, then wheeled it into the curtained cabinet while Houdini thumped and hollered inside to prove he was still there.

"Now then," called Bess, stepping into the cabinet with the trunk. "I shall clap my hands three times . . . I ask you to watch closely for the― effect." At the third clap, she whisked the curtain closed. Assistant and trunk disappeared behind the fabric. But almost instantly, the curtain opened again, and out stepped Houdini. Volunteers raced to undo the rope and unlock the trunk. The flannel bag was still inside, still tied and sealed with wax—and inside that? Bess. The baffled audience cheered wildly as a member of the committee extended a hand to help Houdini's nimble assistant to her feet.

"Just think over this," Houdini boasted in one of their ads. "The time consumed in making the change is three seconds!"

It was a feat perfectly suited to Bess's quick, slight frame and Houdini's muscular dexterity. The Houdinis' signature act was a spectacle with staying power. The couple performed it together on and off for years, even after Houdini's solo career took off.

A theatrical poster advertising the Houdinis' Metamorphosis act, circa 1895.

Houdinis had devised silent and spoken codes for such occasions—but audiences were convinced.

Dr. Hill's own spirits were high when he tallied the receipts, and soon, the California Concert Company was staging spirit acts in a different town each Sunday.

But the Houdinis' success as fake mediums and mind readers alone couldn't save Hill's operation. In early 1898, the medicine show

Spiritualistic
ENTERTAINMENT

...THE FASHIONABLE EVENT OF THE SEASON...

GIVEN BY

MYSTERIOUS
HARRY
Houdini

The Great Occult Demonstrator

ASSISTED BY

MLLE. BEATRICE
HOUDINI

PSYCROMETRIC ●●●●ARTIST

Greatest seance ever introduced in America.
Every manifestation given under test condi-
tions in full light. Independent Spirit Slate
Writing, between two SEALED SLATES.

$100 REWARD

TO ANY SHERIFF, OFFICER, DETECTIVE
OR PRIVATE INDIVIDUAL
Who will produce a handcuff or leg shackle that
PROF. HOUDINI cannot escape from. It's an
utter impossibility to tie rope, or secure the
Medium so as to prevent the manifestations
from occurring

━ SKEPTICS ━
Most Cordially Invited as a Committee

BRING YOUR OWN ROPE AND HANDCUFFS

collapsed, and the young couple set out on their own, booking small venues where Harry performed escapes and the duo continued to fine-tune their best-known magic act, Metamorphosis, the "greatest and finest Trunk Mystery the world has ever seen."

They didn't banish the "spirits" from the show, though. They also incorporated spectral messages, mind reading, and levitating tables, sometimes billing themselves as "The Great Mystifier" and "The Celebrated Psycrometric Clairvoyant."

"I appreciated the fact that I surprised my clients," Houdini later wrote, "but while aware of the fact that I was *deceiving* them I did not see or understand the seriousness." For the time being, he approached the work in a spirit of play. He was living "like a king," after all, compared to life before séances and mind reading, earning much-needed income by posing as a channel between the living and the dead.

Above: Undated advertisement for the Houdinis' early spiritualist act.

Right: Harry and Bess Houdini with the Welsh Brothers Circus, 1895.

The Houdinis spent several more years performing a mishmash of routines in small circuses, music halls, and dime museums (a popular form of "lowbrow" entertainment that brought scientific curiosities and shameless thrills under the same roof). Often changing or renaming their routine as they struggled to find the formula for making it in show business, Harry and Bess had yet to focus and refine the act that would eventually put his talents in the forefront, with Bess stepping back into a supporting role.

By 1899, Houdini was ready to pack it in, give up magic altogether, and resort to teaching others the tricks of his trade. He and Bess moved back to New York to live with his mother, but Harry still had advance bookings to honor, and while performing at a beer

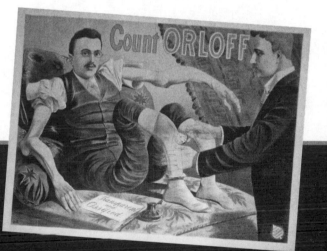

A sideshow poster circa 1885 advertising Count Orloff, the stage name of Ivannow Wladislaus von Dziarski-Orloff (1864–1904), who suffered from an unknown wasting disease that made his skin transparent.

☞ Miraculous Mentors

During Houdini's hungry years on the dime museum circuit, he formed lasting friendships with many of the "freaks"—stars like Count Orloff, the Transparent Man or Human Window Pane ("You Can See His Heart Beat! You Can See His Blood Circulate!")—who attracted big crowds and bigger salaries. In his 1920 book, *Miracle Mongers and Their Methods*, Houdini pays tribute to fire-eaters, glass chewers, sword-, stone-, and umbrella-swallowers, and "defiers of poisonous reptiles," performers like the Incombustible Spaniard, the Human Ostrich, and the Electric Girl. "The dime museum is but a memory now," he wrote. In three generations he believed it would be completely forgotten. Bess often refused to play the dime museums; vaudeville offered more money, stability, and respectability for the young couple. But Houdini learned some handy tricks there hall in St. Paul, Minnesota, he got the break performers dream of. A big-shot manager, vaudeville tycoon Martin Beck, saw his routine and challenged Houdini to escape from a series of handcuffs.

Houdini proved himself with gusto, and on March 14, Beck sent a telegram from Chicago: "You can open Omaha March twenty sixth sixty dollars, will see act probably make you proposition for all next season."

Houdini kept the telegram and later scribbled on it for posterity: "This wire changed my whole Life's journey."

In a year's time, he would be on his way to becoming a household name, a famed star of American entertainment . . . but certainly not as a mind-reading spirit conjurer.

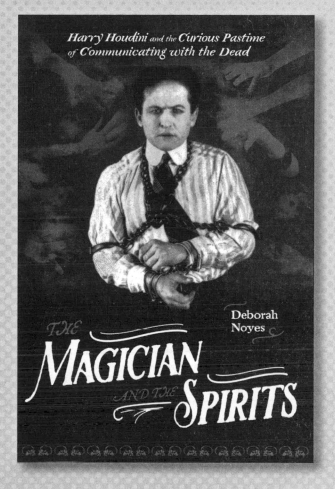

Harry Houdini *and the* Curious Pastime *of* Communicating *with the* Dead

Deborah Noyes

THE

MAGICIAN

AND THE

SPIRITS